THE TET OFFENSIVE AND THE SIEGE OF KHE SANH

by
James Arnold
and
Gordon Rottman

The Tet Offensive and the Siege of Khe Sanh

* A combined volume specially bound for the Veterans of Foreign Wars of the United States through TN Marketing L.L.C.

* Made up of:

Campaign 4 Tet Offensive 1968, by James Arnold

Campaign 150 Khe Sanh 1967-68, by Gordon Rottman

This edition created in 2006 for TN Marketing L.L.C. by Osprey Publishing Ltd.

Contains material first published in Great Britain by Osprey Publishing Ltd, Midland House, West Way, Botley, Oxford, OX2 0PH as Campaign 4 Tet Offensive 1968, by James Arnold, © 1990 Osprey Publishing Ltd; and Campaign 150 Khe Sanh 1967-68, by Gordon Rottman, © 2005 Osprey Publishing Ltd.

Printed in the United States of America.

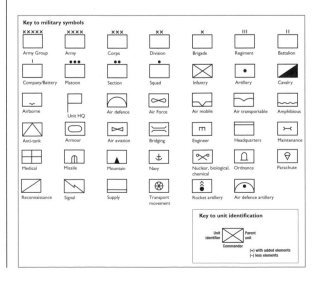

406 West 34th Street
Kansas City, MO 64111

CONTENTS

PART 1

THE TET OFFENSIVE 1968

BACKGROUND TO SURPRISE

The supreme command for the Viet Cong/North Vietnamese Army (VC/NVA) forces had a coherent strategy for conquering South Vietnam that the Americans neither fully appreciated nor effectively countered. In general terms, Communist strategists followed Mao Tse-tung's principles of guerrilla war. But ever inventive, the Vietnamese Communists adapted strategies for their unique circumstances. It was a strategy devised in the early 1960s when America only had advisers in Vietnam, and tenaciously clung to during the difficult years of massive US military activity until final victory. In essence it proved a war-winning strategy.

The overriding goal was to effect a withdrawal of American forces from South Vietnam to bring about negotiations leading to a new, Communist dominated government in the south. To achieve this political end, the National Liberation Front fought on three fronts: political, military, and diplomatic. The political battle involved mobilizing support from the people of South Vietnam while undermining the South Vietnamese government. The military component required confronting the Americans and their allies on the battlefield to inflict losses whenever possible. On the battlefield there were no objectives that had to be

According to Westmoreland's strategy, US forces were to engage regular enemy formations while ARVN forces concentrated on pacification. The problem was finding the enemy. Men of the 1st Cavalry Division (Airmobile) – the élite "First Team" – conduct combat assault into the An Lao Valley.

During the months leading up to the Tet Offensive, President Lyndon Johnson and his administration told the American public that the Allies were winning the war. This left the public unbraced for the coming shock. A well-intentioned man, Johnson lacked the vision to guide the country to a satisfactory resolution of the war. Here he shakes hands during a visit to a hospital at Cam Ranh Bay in 1967.

held. The diplomatic element of the three-prong strategy focused on mobilizing international opposition to the American war effort and promoting anti-war sentiment in the United States. As explained by a high-ranking Viet Cong:

"Every military clash, every demonstration, every propaganda appeal was seen as part of an integrated whole; each had consequences far beyond its immediately apparent results. It was a framework that allowed us to view battles as psychological events."

In mid-1967, the Communist high command decided that the time was ripe for the crowning psychological event, a surprise nationwide offensive to coincide with the Tet holidays.

About the time when Communist planning for the Tet Offensive began, top-level American civilian and military planners met in Honolulu. The conference focused on how to interdict the flow of enemy troops and material into South Vietnam. Inevitably, this led to consideration of higher strategy. The conference's final report stated: "A clear, concise statement of US strategy in Vietnam could not be established … A war of attrition provides neither economy of force nor any foreseeable end to the war." The conference could simply not identify anything worthy of being called a strategy.

In the broadest terms, the American high command had pursued a two-part scheme since 1966. General William C. Westmoreland described this approach in an interview as the Tet Offensive was winding down: "… the [South] Vietnamese forces would concentrate on providing security to the populated areas, while the US forces would provide a shield behind which pacification could be carried out." The idea was that the American forces would operate away from populated areas where they could use their superior firepower and mobility to counter the North Vietnamese Army and Viet Cong mainforce units. Speaking after the war, Marine Corps historian and Vietnam veteran Brigadier General Edwin Simmons commented:

"It's true we violated many of the basic principles of war. We had no clear objective. We had no unity of command. We never had the initiative. The most common phrase was 'reaction force' – we were reacting to them. Our forces were divided and diffused. Since we didn't have a clear objective, we had to measure our performance by statistics."

Thus the sterile tabulation of "Battalion Days in the Field," hamlets "controlled," or most notably "body count" replaced clear strategic direction.

President Lyndon Johnson tried to counter the growing public doubts about the war by a carefully crafted propaganda campaign in late 1967. It claimed that the Communists were slowly losing the war. He sought to gain support for a long-term, limited-war policy. With hindsight it is clear that this approach contained neither a decisive war-winning strategy nor a plausible diplomatic outcome. Worse, from the administration's standpoint, the implicit message was that there would be no unexpected battlefield surprises.

THE PLAN IS BORN

In July 1967, the Communist high command, including political and military leaders from both North and South Vietnam, met in Hanoi. Because North Vietnam recalled its foreign ambassadors to attend the meeting, American intelligence learned of the unusual gathering. It could have been the first piece in the intelligence puzzle leading to anticipation of the coming offensive. Instead, analysts believed the meeting's purpose was to consider a peace bid.

Reviewing events, the Communist leaders recognized that heretofore their battlefield strategy had relied upon well-planned, periodic small- to medium-sized surgical strikes against selected targets and daily small-scale actions designed to raise the enemy's anxiety level and destroy his self-confidence. However, aggressive American tactics during 1967 seemed to auger poorly for the future. A Viet Cong general explains:

"In the spring of 1967 Westmoreland began his second campaign. It was very fierce. Certain of our people were very discouraged. There was much discussion on the course of the war – should we continue main-force efforts, or should we pull back into a more local strategy. But by the middle of 1967 we concluded that you had not reversed the balance of forces on the battlefield. So we decided to carry out one decisive battle to force LBJ to de-escalate the war."

While this statement was written with hindsight, it is doubtful if strategists believed that they could force an American de-escalation so readily. It is notable that aggressive American tactics were producing results and prompted Hanoi to take a huge gamble.

In the summer of 1967 North Vietnamese warriors and diplomats met in Hanoi and decided to take an immense strategic gamble. While the Tet Offensive was Defense Minister Giap's brainchild, Ho Chi Minh gave his blessings to the effort. His recorded tapes were meant to be played on captured South Vietnamese radio stations. Communist planners believed that everyone would rally to the popular "Uncle Ho" and help drive out the hated foreigners.

Impatient and concerned over the trend of events, General Vo Nguyen Giap, the North Vietnamese Defense Minister, proposed a general offensive. While it is difficult to ascertain the high command's exact expectations – as of 1989 they remain obscured by propaganda and the difficulty of gaining access to North Vietnamese records – Giap apparently believed that such an offensive would trigger a popular uprising in the South. Hanoi labeled the plan "the general offensive/ general uprising" indicating that they clearly believed that civilians in the South would rally to their cause. Giap further proposed that the offensive take place during the next lunar New Year festival, some six months hence. The slow, tortuous progress with which supplies could

THE TUNNELS OF CU CHI

Cut-away diagram of Viet Cong underground storage and assembly complex.

US mechanized team
searching for VC

B

AIR SHAFT

Twenty miles northwest of Saigon was the Iron Triangle and the adjacent Cu Chi district. Here, since 1945, the Viet Cong and their village sympathizers had labored to construct an incredible maze of multi-layered, many chambered tunnels. Its existence was a matter of geology, geography, and tactics. The soil itself, laterite clay, was ideal for tunneling since it did not crumble and formed a brick-hard, impermeable surface. The tunnels served as a storage and assembly area. Via a geographic oddity, a protruding finger of Cambodia pointed toward the Iron Triangle and Saigon. Munitions and infiltrating guerrillas moved from sanctuaries in Cambodia to the secure, concealed assembly areas in the tunnels. Allied strategists well understood this and viewed the Iron Triangle as a dagger pointed at Saigon. However, they failed to appreciate the tactical importance of the tunnels. They had a higher purpose than mere concealment. Communist doctrine decreed: "If the tunnels are dug so as to exploit their effectiveness fully, the villages and hamlets will become extremely strong fortresses. The enemy may be several times superior to us in strength and modern weapons, but he will not chase us from the battlefield, because we will launch surprise attacks from within the underground tunnels." Until well past Tet this proved to be exactly the way the VC operated from the tunnels.

The Americans aimed several large-scale search and destroy operations at the Iron Triangle, the best known of which, Operation "Cedar Falls," employed more than 30,000 troops. Literally on the surface, these operations were complete successes: mechanized forces with heavy infantry escorts dominated the above-ground terrain. American officers failed to realize that the absence of the enemy merely meant that he had disappeared underground. The US Army claimed to have destroyed 525 tunnels during "Cedar Falls," yet the local Viet Cong tunnel inspector noted that only the first 50 meters, at most, of any tunnel was damaged. Given that one village had a 1,700-meter long tunnel system, such destruction was hardly paralyzing. In sum, the sweeps through the Iron Triangle disrupted the Viet Cong, but that is all. As soon as the Americans left, the VC resumed their normal routines. As 1967 drew to a close an important part of this routine involved stockpiling resources for the coming offensive.

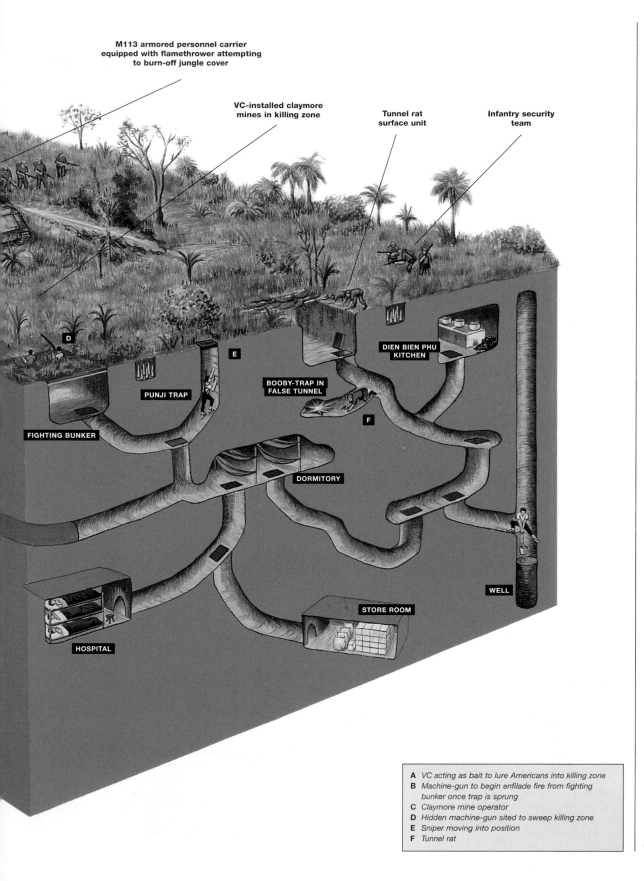

M113 armored personnel carrier
equipped with flamethrower attempting
to burn-off jungle cover

VC-installed claymore
mines in killing zone

Tunnel rat
surface unit

Infantry security
team

D

E

DIEN BIEN PHU
KITCHEN

PUNJI TRAP

BOOBY-TRAP IN
FALSE TUNNEL

F

FIGHTING BUNKER

DORMITORY

WELL

HOSPITAL

STORE ROOM

A VC acting as bait to lure Americans into killing zone
B Machine-gun to begin enfilade fire from fighting
   bunker once trap is sprung
C Claymore mine operator
D Hidden machine-gun sited to sweep killing zone
E Sniper moving into position
F Tunnel rat

move south dictated this long lead time. While the sacrilege of attacking during Tet might offend many Vietnamese, Giap believed the festival would provide the perfect cover. Furthermore, it had an historic precedent: in 1789 Vietnamese patriots had attacked the occupying Chinese in Hanoi during the lunar New Year festival.

To encourage the fighters in the South, the Communist Party utilized all its formidable propaganda powers. Typical was the exhortation given by the Binh Dinh Province Committee to its trusted cadres:

"The General Offensive will occur only once every 1,000 years.

It will decide the fate of the country.

It will end the war.

It constitutes the wishes of both the Party and the people."

At secret bases inside South Vietnam and in adjacent, so-called neutral Laos and Cambodia, morale-building efforts proceeded. The "Second Congress of Heroes, Emulation Combatants and Valiant Men of the South Vietnam People's Liberation Armed Forces" convened to hear Ho Chi Minh's message calling them the "flowers of the nation." They included a one-armed soldier who had learned to fire his rifle with his elbow and killed two Americans, and a mine-laying specialist who had been credited with the implausible total of 400 enemy killed, thus earning the title "Valiant American Killer." One 17-year-old "hero" addressed the meeting: "If he has hatred, even a child can kill Americans." Such efforts as these rekindled flagging Viet Cong spirits.

The offensive required a long lead time because of the difficulty of moving supplies south along the tortuous Ho Chi Minh Trail. This section of the supply line consists of a road carved into the side of a hill for the movement of light trucks.

A "tunnel rat" of the 173rd Airborne Brigade approaches the remains of an enemy campfire far below the surface in the Iron Triangle.

Not all the Communist leaders shared the general euphoria. The deputy political chief for Saigon was in closer touch with reality than his higher command. He knew the urban guerrillas were poorly organized and relatively few in number. When he mentioned his doubts, his superiors dressed him down for being "overly pessimistic" and told him to leave strategy-making to his betters.

In general terms, the July conference in Hanoi decreed that the Tet General Offensive would carry the fighting into previously untouched South Vietnamese urban centers. Here the people would rally to the National Liberation Front and overthrow Thieu's government. Since 1968 was also an election year in America, the successful offensive would help convince the American public that the war was unwinnable. A strike on Saigon was one of the key aspects of the general offensive.

Just as in the Second World War when the German Army secretly advanced through a series of staging areas to surprise the American defenders in the Ardennes, so the Viet Cong brought munitions over the border from Cambodia to the tunnels of Cu Chi and the Iron Triangle. Men and weapons assembled in the tunnels where they received detailed briefings. Systematically they moved into Saigon suburbs and on the eve of the assault gathered in specially prepared safe houses inside Saigon. Agents, often women and children, moved weapons past the city's checkpoints by a variety of subterfuges including hiding them beneath agricultural produce or concealing them inside coffins as part of bogus funeral processions.

Mai Chi Tho, the political commissar of the region encompassing Saigon, carefully planned the assault from a tunnel base in the Iron Triangle:

"During the Tet Offensive, I was in the Iron Triangle. We were working day and night. It was a time of very secret and intensive activity. Many of our officers had to secretly reconnoiter the enemy targets. They moved around in Saigon on forged identity papers. Our fifth columnists, soldiers and officers working inside enemy military installations, came to report."

From such reports, the Viet Cong received detailed information on the defenses they would confront.

The Tet Offensive bore the unmistakable imprint of General Giap. Giap pursued a three-phase military strategy: resistance; general offensive; and general uprising. The strategy featured an evolution from hit and run guerrilla warfare to the formation of regular units that would engage in conventional, objective-seizing battle. The problem with this doctrine was that it required battlefield concentration and thus provided an unmistakable target for American firepower.

Communist planners hoped to utilize captured resources in a variety of imaginative ways. NVA artillerymen were to accompany the assault against an Army of the Republic of Vietnam (ARVN) artillery installation in the central highlands. They would man the captured artillery pieces. Similarly, in Saigon, NVA tank troops would follow the assault against an ARVN armor school to operate the captured vehicles. Near Saigon another artillery team would man weapons captured from an artillery training school. Thus the Communist planners boldly schemed to provide their soldiers with the heavy weapons they had always lacked. Meanwhile, another team carried a recorded speech from Ho Chi Minh designed to promote a popular uprising against the South Vietnamese government. They planned on broadcasting this speech once the assault troops had captured the South Vietnamese national radio station.

CHRONOLOGY

1967

7 July Decision in Hanoi to launch the General Offensive/General Uprising.
Late July Viet Cong leaders meet in Cambodia to plan how to implement the offensive.
29 July Detroit Riots, 15,339 federal and national guard troops sent to Detroit.
7 August Army Chief of Staff reports "smell of success" surrounds Allied effort; beginning of Johnson administration propaganda campaign.
21–3 October Pentagon Riots; three battalions backed by tear gas repulse civilian stone- and bottle-throwing assault.
21 November General Westmoreland predicts US troop withdrawals to start in two years.
15 December Responsibility for Saigon's defense passes to ARVN.
20 December Westmoreland warns Washington of Communists' decision to attempt countrywide war-winning offensive.

1968

10 January Westmoreland orders US pullback to positions closer to Saigon.
20 January Siege of Khe Sanh begins.
23 January North Korea seizes USS *Pueblo*.
29 January Tet holiday cease-fire begins for Allies.
30 January Communists launch premature attack in I and II Corps areas.
31 January Nationwide Communist offensive begins.

The beginning of the large search and destroy missions in 1967, with their attendant increase in American casualties, coincided with a large increase in racial and civil unrest in the USA. During the first nine months of 1967, public anti-war protest, ranging from minor demonstrations to full-scale riots, occurred in 150 cities. These events drained military resources. The October 1967 demonstration in Washington, DC, shown here, culminated in the Pentagon Riots. Over 10,000 Marines and Army troops manned positions inside the nation's capital. Three battalions guarded the Pentagon itself. Military planners had to consider seriously the possibility of national insurrection. Such results justified the North Vietnamese emphasis upon relating battlefield events and American public opinion.

8 February NVA tanks overrun Lang Vei, outside Khe Sanh. Elsewhere, VC/NVA hold only Saigon suburbs and Hue citadel.

13 February Gallup poll reports 50 percent disapprove of Johnson's handling of the war.

17 February Record weekly total of US casualties set during preceding seven days; 543 killed, 2,547 wounded.

18 February 45 cities and bases shelled but only four ground attacks.

21 February COSVN orders a pullback and return to harassing tactics.

24 February Hue's Imperial Palace recaptured.

27 February CBS's Walter Cronkite tells nation that negotiation is the only way out of the war.

1 March US Secretary of Defense Robert McNamara replaced.

10 March *New York Times* reports Westmoreland wants another 206,000 men.

12 March Eugene McCarthy wins 42 percent of vote in New Hampshire Democratic primary election.

16–20 March Gallup poll finds more doves than hawks for first time.

20 March NVA pressure against Khe Sanh diminishes.

22 March Johnson announces Westmoreland will become Army Chief of Staff in mid-1968.

26 March Johnson's special advisers report country has lost confidence in war and that US should disengage.

31 March President Johnson announces partial bombing pause, willingness to negotiate and decision not to run for re-election.

16 April Pentagon announces a gradual policy change to return ARVN forces to the forefront of combat, the origin of "Vietnamization."

3 July Westmoreland replaced by Abrams.

1969

8 June First US troop withdrawal announced.

1972

30 March Communists launch first nationwide offensive since 1968. Much hard fighting. Backed by US airpower, ARVN wins out.

1973

29 March Last US troops withdraw.

1975

30 April NVA tanks spearhead capture of Saigon. South Vietnam surrenders.

1982

11 November Vietnam veterans memorial opens, healing the still-divisive scar of war.

MEN, WEAPONS, AND TACTICS

THE ARMY OF THE REPUBLIC OF VIETNAM

Paratroopers of the élite ARVN Airborne served as a fire brigade force. The 1st and 8th Battalions, intended for movement north as part of Westmoreland's counter to the NVA buildup along the DMZ, were still in Saigon when the Communists struck. Their fortuitous presence gave the Allied commanders an invaluable hard-fighting reaction force. During Tet, airborne troopers rushed from one emergency to the next.

Vietnam has a long tradition of resisting outside influence. Opposition to foreigners superseded internecine dispute. Thus, from the beginning it was an unnatural and very uneasy alliance between the South Vietnamese government and the United States. Moreover, what the South Vietnamese government decreed might well be ignored by a people faced with the options of allying with foreigners to fight their own people, staying neutral, or doing whatever it took to survive. Since 1965 American forces had carried the brunt of offensive operations while the South Vietnamese carried out so-called pacification efforts. Thus, on the eve of Tet, they were dispersed in myriad garrisons scattered around the countryside.

Before Tet the South Vietnamese armed forces included 342,951 regulars in the Army, Navy, Air Force, and Marine Corps. Americans performed most technical and command and control functions in these units. Underpinning the ARVN infantry were some 12,000 American advisers. Each division had about 300 Americans who served as liaison/advisory/logistics specialists. In the field, each battalion had a three- to five-man American advisory team. Since the Americans brought their own radios, they could rapidly tap into the American arsenal of on-call firepower.

In theory, the American assumption of major combat provided a break from the fighting and thus an opportunity for the South Vietnamese to train and improve. In some cases this is what happened. Nha Trang's excellent Dong De (sergeants' school) is a case in point. More often, soldiers sent to training schools naturally took advantage of the respite from combat to loaf. Furthermore, much of the instruction was poor. A veteran infantryman recalls that Ranger school featured instruction based on outdated US Second World War and Korean War doctrine. Some of the instructors were

17

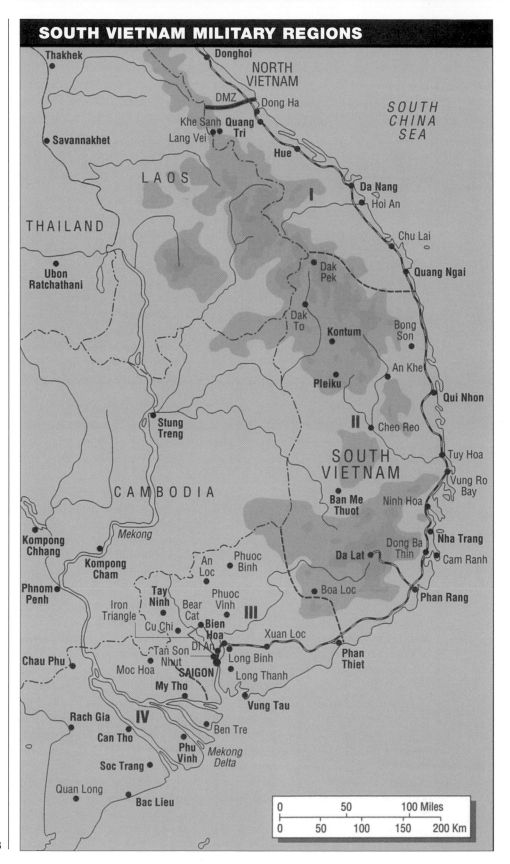

SOUTH VIETNAM MILITARY REGIONS

Thakhek

Donghoi

NORTH
VIETNAM

DMZ

Dong Ha

Khe Sanh Quang
Tri

Savannakhet

Lang Vei

Hue

SOUTH
CHINA
SEA

LAOS

I

Da Nang

Hoi An

THAILAND

Chu Lai

Ubon
Ratchathani

Dak
Pek

Quang Ngai

Dak
To

Kontum

Bong
Son

An Khe

Pleiku

Qui Nhon

Stung
Treng

II

Cheo Reo

Tuy Hoa

SOUTH
VIETNAM

Vung Ro
Bay

CAMBODIA

Ban Me
Thuot

Ninh Hoa

Kompong
Chhang

Mekong

Da Lat

Dong Ba
Thin

Nha Trang

Cam Ranh

Kompong
Cham

An
Loc

Phuoc
Binh

Boa Loc

Phan Rang

Phnom
Penh

Tay
Ninh

Bear
Cat

Phuoc
Vinh

III

Iron
Triangle

Cu Chi

Bien
Hoa

Xuan Loc

Di An

Chau Phu

Tan Son
Nhut

Long Binh

Phan
Thiet

Moc Hoa

SAIGON

Long Thanh

My Tho

Vung Tau

Rach Gia

IV

Ben Tre

Can Tho

Phu
Vinh

Mekong
Delta

Soc Trang

Quan Long

Bac Lieu

0		50		100 Miles
0	50	100	150	200 Km

political appointees. The key instructor position was a patronage post, a welcome, comfortable rear-area assignment. Too often instructors taught American doctrine by rote. In contrast were wounded veterans who would not deal with obsolete doctrine; instead "they taught wisdom."

Ironically, by the time the combat schools had updated their curriculum to teach counterinsurgency, the enemy had switched to more conventional, mainforce tactics. Ranger School's "muddy diploma" – so called because most graduates attended during the monsoon season when combat was at an ebb – and much of the other instruction that was supposed to take place while Americans bore the brunt of combat, failed to achieve American expectations. Part of the problem stemmed from poor equipment. Most ARVN units lacked modern radios, essential for calling artillery and air support. Before Tet, only the élite Airborne battalions and Marine Brigade, one infantry regiment, and five Ranger battalions possessed M-16 rifles. The balance of the ten regular infantry divisions and virtually all the various militias made do with assorted outdated weapons. These units knew they were outgunned when confronting AK-47-firing North Vietnamese regulars or mainforce Viet Cong.

Endemic corruption afflicted many units. Thieu's spoils system kept him securely in power by awarding command positions to cronies, but combat leadership suffered. The common soldier knew that all too often his officers enriched themselves on US aid meant to increase their fighting ability. This situation prevailed even among so-called élite units. Periodically, Westmoreland had to threaten to withhold funds from Ranger battalions, supposedly among the army's best, because they were absconding with massive amounts of aid intended for the civilians they were protecting.

When examining the pre-Tet ARVN order of battle, American planners saw a very uneven picture of performance. Some ARVN units had benefited from withdrawal from front-line combat. Others had lost all combat effectiveness. There were some excellent units, most notably the airborne and marine units. An American adviser said of them:

ALLIED ORDER OF BATTLE

US FORCES AND STRENGTHS, JANUARY 31, 1968
Divisions
1st Marine Division (22,466)
3rd Marine Division (24,417)
1st Cavalry Division (18,647) (the Army's best)
1st Infantry Division (17,539)
4th Infantry Division (19,042)
9th Infantry Division (16,153)
23rd (American) Division (15,825) (newly formed)
25th Infantry Division (17,666)
101st Airborne Division (15,220) (airborne in name only)

Brigades and Other Units
173rd Airborne Brigade (5,313)
199th Infantry Brigade (4,215)
11th Armored Cavalry Regiment (4,331)
5th Special Forces Group (Airborne) (3,400)

Summary
79 Army battalions, 23 Marine battalions, 3,100 helicopters

Allied Forces
1st Australian Task Force (three battalions, about 6,000)

Royal Thai Army Volunteer Regiment (Queen's Cobras) (about 2,400)
Capital (Tiger) Infantry Division (Korean)
9th (White Horse) Division (Korean)
2nd Marine Corps Brigade (Korean)
Authorized Korean manpower: 42,769
Actual pre-Tet strength: 48,800

ARMY REPUBLIC OF SOUTH VIETNAM
Airborne Division (élite)
Marine Corps (two solid 3-battalion brigades)
1st Division (the best regular division)
2nd Division (problem-prone, high desertion)
5th Division (barely effective)
7th Division (barely effective)
9th Division (the Army's poorest)
18th Division (combat-ineffective)
21st Division (a good division)
22nd Division (adequate, improving)
23rd Division (adequate, improving)
25th Division (improved after receiving M-16s)
Ranger Battalions (uneven, from very good to poor)
Regional Forces (151,376 militia)
Popular Forces (148,789 militia)
Civilian Irregular Defense Groups (42,000 militia)

Total Allied Forces as of December 31, 1967: 1,298,000

A soldier of the 5th Marine Battalion holds a VC 75mm recoilless rifle round.

"These guys are part of the strategic reserve. They get moved all over the country to fight and are away from their families 10 or 11 months a year, year after year. They are all volunteers. When people say the South Vietnamese won't fight, they shouldn't include units like the Vietnamese Marines."

However, in the American estimation, corruption and poor training, leadership, and equipment rendered six of the ten regular divisions combat ineffective.

At the bottom of the pecking order of Allied units were the 42,000 men comprising the Civilian Irregular Defense Groups (CIDG). The task of training and leading these groups fell to the American and Vietnamese Special Forces. There were two categories of CIDG: Camp Strike Forces (CSF) and Mobile Strike Forces (MSF, familiarly known as "Mike Forces"). The former garrisoned the Special Forces' camps while the latter comprised the better trained soldiers (a relative term) capable of active patrolling. A battalion of CSF soldiers, three to five 132-man companies, guarded each camp. Their families usually lived in an adjacent American-built slum put together with nipa palm and stolen materials. In remote situations these camps existed in isolation from normal regional life; in more populous areas they became a center for people seeking a safe haven. Since one of the goals of the coming offensive was to prove to the people that the South Vietnamese government and its allies could not protect its citizens, the CIDG camps were included on the target list.

The CIDG had limited capabilities. They were at the bottom of the hierarchy for supplies, medical evacuation, fire support, and everything else. Most of their training came from field experience facing "real" training aids who shot back with superior weapons. However, molded by the Green Berets, they sometimes accomplished surprising feats. A Special Forces officer has left a description of his men on the eve of Tet:

1st ARVN Division radiomen and their American advisers coordinate operations with a nearby American Fire Support Base.

A CIDG platoon at its base in the II Corps hinterland. Note the many young teenagers that make up this force.

US infantryman. Illustration by Richard Geiger

"These CIDGs were soldiers who would cut up their canteen covers to make green fur collars for their uniforms; who could struggle all day through thigh-deep mud, carrying half their own weight on their backs without complaint ... who would bang two B-40 rockets together like indian clubs to see if they would explode ... who might run under fire; or who might ignore it to carry a wounded American to safety."

Except for selected CIDG camps, the Communist assault tended to bypass rural areas in favor of city assaults. Thus, the 151,376-man Regional Forces and 148,789-man Popular Forces played a limited part in the Tet Offensive. In the cities the attackers confronted the 70,000-man Vietnamese national police who were forced to play a combat role with which they were unfamiliar and for which they were ill prepared.

THE AMERICAN INFANTRY

On the eve of Tet, US forces comprised nine divisions, one armored cavalry regiment, and two independent brigades. This force had 100 infantry and mechanized battalions numbering 331,098 Army soldiers and 78,013 Marines. The most aggressive of these troops, the Marines, 1st Cavalry Division, 173rd Airborne Brigade, and 11th Armored Cavalry Regiment, were the equal of any of the crack American formations that participated in the two World Wars. The

The M-16 was the basic and controversial firearm of the US foot soldier. An automatic rifle, on full automatic it delivered its 20-round magazine in three seconds. To reduce the likelihood of jamming, many soldiers only loaded 18 rounds. Still the M-16 had to be meticulously maintained or else it jammed. The relative merits of the rival automatic rifles were much debated. One VC company commander stated: "The AK-47 was a good weapon, but most of us carried M-16s." Asked why, he responded: "It was so much easier to get ammunition. You were always dropping magazines full of it, or we could buy it from the puppet (South Vietnamese) forces." A Marine belonging to "A" Company, 1/1 Marine Regiment, during the Battle of Hue, February 9, 1968.

balance were dependable, if unexceptional, soldiers willing to perform their duty.

Writing with the advantage of hindsight, an American officer commented that his country did not acquire ten years' experience in Vietnam, but rather had "one year's experience ten times." The reason for this was the rotation system under which a soldier served a twelve-month tour of duty. Every soldier knew to the day his personal DEROS (Date Expected Return Overseas). Most soldiers' prime motivation was to

Every squad included a soldier armed with the M-79 grenade launcher. The M-79 was a single-shot, break-open, breech-loaded shoulder weapon. When loaded it weighed 6.5 pounds. It fired a 40mm grenade to an effective range of 400 yards (while the maximum range of a hand-lobbed grenade was 40 yards). It had a sustained rate of aimed fire of five to seven rounds per minute. Grenadiers carried ammunition in specially designed, pouch-lined jackets. The effectiveness of the "blooper" gunners made them, along with the radiomen, the first targets in an ambush. A VC captain commented: "We were very frightened of it ... A terrible weapon."

survive until that day. The Vietnam rotation policy differed from previous wars. During the two World Wars soldiers served for the duration. In Korea, rear-echelon troops served longer than those in combat units. In Vietnam, everyone served the same tour. Typically, for several weeks following arrival in country, a soldier was excited and perhaps looked forward to combat. He lost this enthusiasm after his first engagement. From about the second to the eighth month he performed his combat role dutifully. Then he began to consider himself an "old soldier" and, like all such, became reluctant to take risks. Often, as a soldier neared his DEROS, sympathetic officers gave him a more secure assignment.

The rotation policy had a major impact on how America fought the war. Rapid manpower turnover hindered the development of *esprit de corps*. There was a constant influx of green troops replacing combat experienced men. Since the likelihood of encountering the enemy was somewhat random, a newly arrived soldier had about the same chance of engaging in hard combat as did an experienced soldier. A North Vietnamese officer commenting on why America lost said: "One weak point was your rotation of soldiers. You were strangers here anyway, and as soon as someone began to learn the country you sent him home." Thus,

LEFT **Vertical envelopment, landing troops via helicopter behind enemy lines, was a new military concept, first applied during the Vietnam War. In 1965 and 1966, when the Communists first confronted this new weapon, they were taken by surprise and slaughtered in droves. But the helicopter was a mixed blessing. A North Vietnamese general who commanded in the first battles against the US 1st Cavalry Division commented: "With your helicopters you could strike deep into our rear without warning. It was very effective." However, "We were amazed at how dependent you were on helicopters." The helicopter gave the illusion of control. Troops could land anywhere the terrain permitted, deep within enemy-dominated territory. But once they departed the land reverted to the enemy.**

ABOVE RIGHT **The gunner's view. in this case friendly soldiers of the 1st ARVN Division sweeping through a hamlet. When targets could be seen, the helicopter gave the Allies what in wars past had been called the "high ground."**

from the soldiers' standpoint, the major morale factor was the rotation policy. He knew the war would not be won during his tour of duty, so he reasonably asked "why try?" His patriotic and self-sacrificial tendencies competed with instincts for self-preservation. For him: "The end of the war was marked by the individual's rotation date and not by the war's eventual outcome –whether victory or defeat."

The rotation policy also had an adverse impact on the officer corps. Knowing their time was limited, many officers selfishly sought to

As in most wars, there was not a "typical" soldier on either side. Because of the difficult jungle terrain, field expedients ruled the day. An American foot soldier going on patrol might carry a rucksack stuffed with basic equipment weighing some 50 pounds. In addition, he hefted three days' rations, 500 M-16 rifle rounds, four one-pound fragmentation grenades, two smoke grenades, one or two Claymore mines, 200 rounds for his unit's M-60 machine-gun, three or four canteens of water and his individual weapon. Here, 1st Infantry Division soldiers take a break from a tracking patrol.

Flying from bases in Guam, the B-52 bomber – originally designed for strategic nuclear attack – served as a conventional ground support bomber in South Vietnam. It carried a colossal bomb load, up to 84 750-pound bombs, that could be dropped as close as one kilometer from friendly troops. The B-52 flew so high that it could not be heard on the ground: thus in theory they struck without warning. However, Soviet vessels stationed near the B-52 bases, spies' reports from the heavily infiltrated South Vietnamese command, and careless American security measures frequently gave the intended target advance warning. None the less, B-52 carpet bombing attacks could be devastating and greatly contributed to the defense of Khe Sanh.

enhance their careers during their Vietnam service. This was the infamous "ticket punching" behavior so criticized after the war. The officer's goal was not to win the war, but to acquire a good fitness report for his file. Furthermore, career officers strove to serve six months in a combat unit and six in a staff position. This combined experience gave

LEFT Jet strike aircraft provided close support in daylight conditions of good visibility. Because of their speed, the "fast-movers" were hard targets for enemy antiaircraft gunners to hit. Although the Americans used a variety of jet aircraft, the Air Force's F-100 Super Sabre was the most common jet used in South Vietnam. It carried up to 6,000 pounds of ordnance.

RIGHT Typical soldier of the Viet Cong. Illustration by Mike Chappell.

them the best chance for future promotion. Yet it had a serious adverse impact on operations in the field. Just about the time an officer became experienced enough to lead effectively, he switched jobs. A new commander brought new procedures, and everyone constantly had to change, adjust, and relearn all aspects of combat. This was a serious disadvantage, particularly against a foe who had fought a lifetime on the same ground.

The fundamental military challenge confronting the Americans and their allies was that, despite unprecedented mobility provided by helicopters and APCs, they infrequently contacted the enemy unless he wanted the contact. The Tet Offensive changed this. The enemy massed his forces and tried to hold his ground.

THE COMMUNISTS

Communist forces fell into two distinct groups: the North Vietnamese Army (NVA) regulars and the Viet Cong (VC). At the war's beginning, the southern-born Viet Cong operated in true guerrilla style without support from the NVA regulars. As the war intensified, increasing numbers of North Vietnamese made the perilous march south along the Ho Chi Minh Trail to join the fighting. American intelligence estimated that at the time of the offensive, about fifty percent of the 197 mainforce enemy battalions in the south comprised NVA regulars. At all times, the Hanoi high command dominated their southern brethren. The NVA's objective was to reunify Vietnam: the Viet Cong – fighting under the banner of the National Liberation Front – had the slightly different goal of obtaining a monopoly of political power in the south. American intelligence had identified seven North Vietnamese Army divisions in South Vietnam by the beginning of 1968. They numbered about 50,000 soldiers. Additional NVA regulars served in mainforce VC units.

Until the war's end, a North Vietnamese soldier sent south returned home only in one of two circumstances. If he belonged to the small cadre held out of battle to reconstruct a battered unit (a practice similar to that used by assault, troops in the First World War) he would return to escort replacements back south. A disabling wound was the only other ticket home. As the war dragged on, more and more recruits saw orders sending them south as a death sentence. Yet they went, and, in sharp contrast to American policy, the NVA soldier served for the duration. As one envious American general expressed it: "Charlie had no DEROS."

Compared with the Allies, the NVA lived an extremely primitive life. Their health suffered accordingly. A typical NVA prisoner reported that while everyone took malaria pills, due to their poor physical condition, 70 men in his company had contracted the disease by the time of his capture.

It was also a life lacking comfort and pleasure. While during the march south through Laos and Cambodia they occasionally met women at communications and liaison stations, once they neared the combat zone they seldom made contact with the opposite sex. Each evening a political officer harangued the men. He told of combat heroes and of great past and future successes against the ARVN and Americans. Typically, a commissar might acknowledge the strength of American aircraft and guns while stressing the moral superiority of the NVA/VC. Although political indoctrination was an important component of orthodox Communist training, at least one veteran reported that it often failed to stimulate the troops for a most basic reason: the political officer did not accompany the men on combat missions and thus was discredited. Periodically traveling entertainment troops arrived to enliven the soldiers' lonely routine. While their arrival was welcome, particularly if the troop featured women, their departure only highlighted the men's isolation. The life of an NVA soldier was one of tremendous physical and emotional deprivation.

Within the Viet Cong were two levels of combatants: mainforce (called regular by the Americans) units that numbered about 60,000 men organized into regular combat units, and the paramilitary or

The NVA/VC had to confront a battlefield fact of life: they invariably faced vastly superior American firepower. They constantly sought ways to compensate by using every possible stratagem conceivable by a very inventive people. These ranged from pre-battle morale/political indoctrination to post-battle evasion and retreat tactics.

A captured NVA regular wears the characteristic Ho Chi Minh sandals and pith helmet. Heavy Tet losses among southern-born Viet Cong shifted the war's burden to the northern regulars.

guerrilla forces. The latter, in turn, comprised regional, or territorial, guerrillas and local guerrillas. Main force units engaged in full scale combat and were veteran, skilled fighters. The paramilitary units provided logistical support, scouts and guides, and engaged in hit and run ambushes and mine laying. While it is exceedingly difficult to reconstruct the Communist order of battle – it was a source of great debate at the time within Westmoreland's headquarters – on the eve of Tet, some 400,000 paramilitary fighters were present.

The fundamental problems confronting the Communists are well-expressed by the commander of the 2nd Viet Cong Division: "When the Americans entered the war, we spent all our time trying to figure out how to fight you. The incredible density of your firepower and your mobility were our biggest concerns."

COMMUNIST WEAPONS AND TACTICS

Both the Viet Cong and the North Vietnamese lacked the heavy weapons of their opponents. They essentially operated as light infantry. Since they could not compete with American firepower, they developed a variety of compensatory tactics. Analysis of the initial encounters with the Americans led to the following conclusion according to a Viet Cong general: "The way to fight the American was to grab him by his belt, to get so close that his artillery and air power was useless." The Communists had rediscovered the "hugging" tactics used by the Germans during the Second World War.

Secondly, the Communists had to counter American mobility. A North Vietnamese general explains how this was done:

"Our mobility was only our feet, so we had to lure your troops into areas where helicopters and artillery would be of little use. And we tried to turn those advantages against you, to make you so dependent on them that you would never develop the ability to meet us on our terms – on foot, lightly armed, in the jungle."

Often such jungle combats featured the VC/NVA fighting from entrenched positions. If they chose to fight outside fortified areas, the Communists tried to strike hard and fast and then withdraw before American firepower intervened. Usually they sought to engage American units who were moving and were thus more vulnerable. Despite all these tactics, if it came down to a slugging match, the VC/NVA could not compete with American firepower. One NVA combat veteran estimated that 70 to 80 percent of all NVA losses came from artillery and airstrikes.

The NVA/VC always prepared meticulously before launching an assault. Operations typically began with a careful reconnaissance of the objective. The recon unit, comprising the best soldiers, moved close to the Allied position and then dispatched two- or three-man teams to move in as close as possible to scout the objective. The recon unit paid particular attention to the positions of the defenders' heavy weapons. Upon its return to base, the recon unit diagrammed the objective for the sappers who were to spearhead the assault. The sappers were the second most élite soldiers in NVA units. Frequently, assault troops constructed a sand table of the hostile position. Each unit studied the table and then rehearsed its role. In preparation for infiltrating Allied positions, everyone received instruction in disarming mines and trip flares. In actual assaults, élite sapper units led the way. Even the most formidable-seeming positions proved porous against the Communists' skilled infiltration abilities.

For the Tet Offensive, most objectives were in urban areas. A prisoner explained the scouting procedures used here:

"In our reconnaissance of cities, we are normally met by local force liaison people at a prearranged location within or close to the city. The liaison people escort us to the exact positions or locations to be attacked. If there are several ARVN soldiers in the area, we usually disguise ourselves as ARVNs. But in cities where there are only a few ARVN soldiers, we wear civilian clothes."

The Communists took advantage of the Christmas truce for a final reconnaissance. The commander of the 9th Viet Cong Division, for example, personally inspected his unit's primary objective, Tan Son Nhut Air Base outside Saigon, while one of his regimental commanders visited "the family grave site" at a military cemetery just outside the base.

Because the VC/NVA units lacked modern communications, officers could not adjust plans to changing circumstances. Thus assault units received rigid orders to follow the attack plan. A prisoner recounts:

"All units must go by this plan and a soldier must execute an order even if many get killed. They must launch the attack at all costs. The

The AK-47 was the standard hand-held firearm on the Communist side. The Russian-designed gas-operated automatic rifle fired a 762mm round. It had an effective range of 400 meters and delivered 30 rounds per magazine. Ruggedly built, it was believed by many American soldiers to be greatly superior to their own M-16. In contrast to earlier wars where foot soldiers fired rifles, the AK-47 turned every enemy infantryman into a light machine-gunner. A young Viet Cong soldier carries the Chinese version of the AK-47.

plan always shows how to get into the objective area, where key points to be destroyed are located and how best to exfiltrate."

In another tactical departure, many attacking units at Tet had no prepared withdrawal routes. It was a point of discipline and pride always to try to carry away the wounded and the dead. This practice led to the frustrating experience of an Allied unit fighting an intense combat, taking losses, and after the battle finding little to indicate if the enemy, in turn, had suffered.

Regular soldier of the NVA. Illustration by Mike Chappell.

In the absence of artillery, heavy fire support had to come from rockets, recoilless rifles and mortars. Mortars included 82mm and 120mm weapons. The latter type was a most formidable weapon. Based on Soviet design, the 120mm mortar had a range in excess of four miles. A five-man crew served the weapon and could break it down into three loads to carry it through even the most rugged terrain.

The mortar attack had been a staple of Viet Cong tactics since the war began. Relying upon careful reconnaissance, a mission made easier by the near total lack of concealment of important posts within an Allied installation, the mortar crews prepared concealed firing sites and calculated firing angles before the bombardment began.

Thus they were able accurately to "walk" their rounds across a base's important installations in a short, intense bombardment. This bombardment both inflicted losses and forced the defenders to keep their heads down. While the defenders were hunkered down, élite sappers spearheaded the effort to breach the defenses.

Far less accurate were the free-flight 107mm, 122mm, and 140mm rockets. Rockets had figured prominently in Russian Second World War tactics, so it is not surprising that the Russians supplied rockets to their allies. The rocket's great merit was that it efficiently delivered a large explosive charge to the target. A 90-pound rocket, transported in two sections, could be carried to its launching site and propel a 35-pound charge to a target 10 kilometers distant. It required a conventional howitzer weighing some 3,300 pounds to equal this firepower. Thus the rocket had a much superior warhead-to-weight ratio. On the down side, rockets were inaccurate. They were useless for hitting discrete targets. Accordingly, Communist gunners employed rockets as

LEFT **Up until the Tet Offensive, the Viet Cong and North Vietnamese avoided battle except on ground of their own choosing. Usually they tried to draw the Americans into a prepared killing ground that featured well-camouflaged, deeply dug trenches, bunkers, and spider holes. Experienced American officers learned to avoid assaulting unknown numbers of enemy soldiers in prepared positions. Instead, they preferred to fall back and call in air strikes and artillery. However, the imperative to report a sizable "body count" drove some aggressive leaders to costly and foolish attacks. The 173rd Airborne's assault on hill 875 in 1967 and the Hamburger Hill action in 1969 were two dismal examples. A trench/tunnel complex uncovered by the 173rd Airborne Brigade.**

BELOW LEFT
A captured VC sapper reported: "You had lots of wire around Polei Kleng but it was easy to get through. I just don't think you have a defensive barrier that is effective against us." At Hue, a spearheading sapper company formed four 10-man teams equipped with two B40 and one B41 rocket launchers as well as AK and CKZ rifles with 200 rounds of ammunition. Each sapper also carried 20 explosive charges to breach fortified defenses. Nearly naked, to avoid tangling in wire, a former VC sapper demonstrates infiltration technique.

RIGHT **Russian-manufactured rocket propelled grenades (RPGs) were the descendants of the very successful Second World War German hand-held antitank weapons. Nominally effective up to 500 yards, in combat the NVA and VC employed RPGs at much closer range. RPGs could penetrate up to 250mm-thick armor, easily an overmatch for the M-113's 35mm-thick plating. RPGs and rockets took a terrible toll of Marine Corps tank troops during the street fighting in Hue.**

ABOVE **The Soviet RPD machine-gun fired the same ammunition as the American M-60. However, at 10.5 pounds it was less than half as heavy as its counterpart. It was capable of firing 900 meters, 200 meters less than the M-60, but this seldom mattered in situations where combat ranges typically were less than 20 meters.**

area bombardment weapons, particularly against airfields and ammunition dumps, and to deliver sudden, stunning saturation fire to cover an assault. Nationwide, the typical first warning that the Tet Offensive was underway came when mortar rounds and rockets exploded on defensive positions.

Only along the DMZ did the North Vietnamese Army employ tube artillery. In late 1967 it hauled Russian-designed 130mm field guns into fortified firing positions and began the long-range bombardment of Marine positions. To American generals, this was reminiscent of Dien Bien Phu, and was one more factor drawing their attention north as the Communists prepared for the real assault elsewhere.

In spite of this calculus, the Communist high command's plan called for its soldiers to switch their tactics completely. For the first time in the war, they were to capture and hold selected objectives throughout the country. To do this they had to mass – and this would provide unmistakable targets for US firepower.

ON THE EVE

When it was all over, it seemed that American intelligence officers had had the pieces of the puzzle in their hands but had been unable to assemble a clear picture of enemy intent. As early as October 29, 1967, the Viet Cong 273rd Regiment had attacked a small district capital and, contrary to normal practice, tried to hold it. They suffered

terribly when the inevitable massive Allied air and artillery bombardment drove them out. Intelligence officers could not understand why the enemy risked certain heavy losses for a meaningless objective. With hindsight they understood that the Communists were practicing urban assault tactics.

Similarly, in November four NVA regiments fought a bitter 22-day campaign around the obscure border town of Dak To. The Americans redeployed the equivalent of a division to defeat the assault. Captured documents revealed that the attack had been designed to "force the enemy to deploy as many additional troops to the Western Highlands as possible." The scheme worked, though again at heavy cost. The American troops had vacated positions around some of the urban objectives specified for the Tet Offensive.

There were other tell-tale signs: a flurry of attacks in Dinh Tuong Province where historically the Viet Cong tested new tactics; a sharp decline in Communist desertion rates (the troops were being told that victory was near); prisoner statements that the entire country would be "liberated" by Tet. By December 1967, high-ranking American officers had begun to believe that the Communists would try a major offensive in the near future. America's top soldier, General Earle Wheeler, Chairman of the Joint Chiefs of Staff, addressed the US public on December 18, twenty-three years and two days after the surprise German assault in the Ardennes, to say that "there may be a Communist thrust similar to the desperate effort of the Germans in the Battle of the Bulge."

Wheeler's warning came from the analysis performed by Westmoreland and his staff, who had been carefully studying captured documents. These clearly described a change in Communist strategy.

ABOVE **Poor communications forced the Communist attackers to adhere to plans. Such inflexibility caused heavy losses when rapid American countermeasures placed reserves between the attackers and their objectives. In Saigon, in particular, initial Communist successes degenerated into uncoordinated small unit actions. Only at higher command levels did the Communists have field telephones (shown here) and radios.**

RIGHT **A captured 82mm mortar on right stands next to a US 81mm version. The Communists could fire American ammunition even though the tube was slightly larger. Mortar and rocket bombardment heralded most of the initial Tet attacks.**

BELOW **The lightly armed Viet Cong had to find alternatives to compensate for their lack of firepower. They relied heavily upon mines and booby traps. A VC document analyzing American tactics stated: "US troops clumsy and vulnerable to booby trapping and mining." Mines inflicted about half the damage and destruction American armor suffered. Mines and booby traps caused 10 percent of US fatalities and 15 percent of wounds between 1965 and 1970. Furthermore, their presence served as a substantial tactical brake on ground operations. When a trap exploded to kill or maim, the infuriating knowledge that local civilians knew the location of nearby booby traps sometimes drove the survivors to commit savage atrocities.**

Accordingly, the general informed Washington that the Communists intended "to undertake an intensified countrywide effort, perhaps a maximum effort." The administration responded by speeding up the schedule of troop movements to Vietnam, but that was all. Except for Wheeler's statement, which had little impact, the Johnson administration chose not to reveal Westmoreland's analysis to the public and did nothing to brace the American people for the coming blow. Having spent the past months claiming great progress, policy makers – military and civilian alike – refused to reverse course. They persisted in painting a rosy picture and by this decision played right into Giap's hands.

On January 5, the US Mission released documents captured on November 19, 1967, which included an order to the People's Army:

"Use very strong military attacks in coordination with the uprisings of the local population to take over towns and cities. Troops should flood the lowlands. They should move toward liberating the capital city [Saigon]."

Yet the attached analysis provided by the mission, apparently reflecting the prevailing belief in Westmoreland's headquarters, was that these orders were "ambiguous" as to the time fixed for the attack and possibly represented "internal propaganda" designed to inspire the enemy's troops.

When the South Vietnamese General Staff later studied the Tet Offensive they hit upon the essential basis for the intelligence failure. Having been taught American doctrine, they were primarily concerned with the Communist "capabilities and not his intentions." Capabilities could be quantified, and it was clear to all the Allies that the enemy could not hope to capture and hold urban objectives. Therefore, intelligence officers dismissed all indications that the enemy intended to try anyway.

A second major factor beyond the inability of military intelligence to assess accurately the signs of enemy build-up accounts for the Tet Offensive's surprise. When the American high command examined their strategic maps at the beginning of 1968, they focused on the northernmost provinces bordering the so-called demilitarized zone (DMZ) that separated North and South Vietnam. Since mid-1967, Westmoreland had been shuffling strength northward in response to the enemy's growing strength. By the New Year he had positioned a tremendous amount of available military resources there. The positions included a series of fortified, but isolated, Marine Corps posts along the DMZ. The high command, and President Johnson in particular, feared that a major assault across the border and from neighboring Laos might turn one of these bases into a Dien Bien Phu. Mid-January patrol actions seemed to confirm the high command's worries: two dug-in NVA divisions had surrounded the Marine Corps combat base of Khe Sanh. In sum, by January 1968, enemy pressure had over-stretched American resources. Distracted by the threat in the north, the US high command seriously underestimated the enemy's potential for major, nationwide attacks.

An aerial view of Khe Sanh. Communist pressure against this base caused Westmoreland to divert increasing strength to the northern I Corps region. With hindsight, it appears he was duped by a skilful Communist diversionary build-up.

Major General Frederick C. Weyand commanded the American field forces in III Corps Tactical Zone. His command stretched from Saigon out to the Cambodian border. According to Westmoreland's recent strategy, 39 of his 53 maneuver battalions were operating against enemy bases along the Cambodian border. Unbeknown to Weyand, as the Americans shifted out from the urban area, the Communists marched in. However, radio intercepts and the lack of contact with the enemy in the border area alarmed Weyand. On January 9 he telephoned

TOP RIGHT **The basic armored vehicle of the rear was the M-113 armored personnel carrier (APC). Combat experience quickly showed the need to increase the armor and firepower of the APC. Technicians bolted extra armor along the sides to protect against RPGs, belly armor to shield against mines and an armored cupola for the commander's .50cal machine-gun. The addition of two side-mounted M-60 machine-guns converted the vehicle to the Armored Cavalry Assault Vehicle. Mechanized units used the ACAVs as light tanks. They had surprising cross-country ability. The combination of mobility and firepower demonstrated to the high command that armor could usefully contribute to the war. Westmoreland wrote: "The ability of mechanized cavalry to operate effectively in the Vietnamese countryside convinced me that I was mistaken in a belief that modern armor had only a limited role in the fighting in Vietnam."**

BOTTOM RIGHT **By the beginning of 1968, the Allies had assembled a considerable armored force. The US Army's contingent included the famous 11th Armored Cavalry Regiment, seven divisional cavalry squadrons, seven mechanized battalions, two tank battalions, and an independent tank company, and five cavalry troops supporting light infantry and airborne units. The Marine Corps also had considerable armored assets. The crack 1st Australian Task Force provided an APC troop. Ten South Vietnamese armored cavalry squadrons were available.**

RVN National Police Field Force enlisted man, Saigon. Illustration by Mike Chappell.

Westmoreland to explain his concern and to recommend that forces return from the border. In a key decision, Westmoreland agreed. When the Communists struck, the number of American battalions within the urban zone had doubled. Their presence made a tremendous difference.

Elsewhere, as January progressed, disquieting signs of enemy build-up continued and they too prompted countermeasures. Early in the month, the 4th Division in the Central Highlands captured a plan for an attack on

Pleiku. In mid-January, 101st Airborne captured plans for an attack on the province capital of Phu Cuong. However, the Communist practice of compartmentalizing planning paid dividends. Since neither of the plans mentioned anything except the immediate activities of the units involved, American intelligence officers failed to foresee that they were part of a nationwide plan. Consequently, countermeasures were left to local commanders. On January 26 the 4th Division commander, Major General Charles Stone, assembled all area commanders and prepared a coordinated response should an attack take place. His foresight stands in sharp contrast to that of other commanders. He also moved a tank company to Pleiku as a mobile reserve. Similarly, a few days later, Westmoreland ordered the 4th Cavalry Squadron to relocate near Saigon's Tan Son Nhut airbase. He reckoned that "they would provide a ready mobile reserve with impressive firepower." Both of these small shifts helped when the attack came.

By January, Westmoreland had become sufficiently alarmed to request that the South Vietnamese cancel the coming Tet cease-fire. On January 8 the chief of the South Vietnamese Joint General Staff, General Cao Van Vien, told Westmoreland that he would try to limit the truce to 24 hours. A week later, President Thieu argued that to cancel the 48-hour cease-fire would adversely affect his nation and its soldiers. He agreed to limit the cease-fire to 36 hours, beginning on the evening of January 29. The South Vietnamese government promised to announce the change one day before it was to take effect. In the event it failed to make the announcement in a timely, useful way. In the IV Corps region south of Saigon, for example, the order canceling the Tet cease-fire reached headquarters shortly after 10pm, a mere four and a half hours before the attacks began.

ABOVE **General Fred Weyand sensed too many troops were deployed along the Cambodian border. He urged Westmoreland to recall them to positions closer to Saigon. This redeployment proved to be Westmoreland's best decision before Tet.**

BELOW **Major General Charles Stone (back row, third from right) carefully prepared defensive plans in case the Communists struck. His care paid great dividends in the defense of Pleiku.**

The Americans did little better. During the day of January 30 Westmoreland's headquarters issued a warning directing that "Troops will be placed on maximum alert with particular attention to the defense of headquarters complexes, logistical installations, airfields, population centers, and billets." This warning covered the prime targets of the impending assault, yet it either came too late or was largely ignored.

So, heedless of coming crisis, the South Vietnamese prepared to celebrate their lunar New Year. The celebration's peak would come on the night of January 30. The official ARVN history describes the nation's mood:

"A relative lull seemed to be prevailing all over South Vietnam … leaves were readily granted the troops for the lunar New Year and measures were taken by the Administration to give the common people as normal a Tet as possible … The people had forgotten about the dying war. They wanted to celebrate Tet with as much fervor as in the old days."

During the night of January 30 revelers swarmed the streets of Saigon to greet the New Year of the Monkey. Soldiers belonging to the local garrison had not received word the authorities had canceled the truce. But everyone knew that the ban on fireworks had been lifted for the holidays, so the explosions of thousands of traditional fire-crackers rocked the air. Slowly, as Viet Cong assault forces moved from their safehouses into attack position – some of the 67,000 committed nationwide in the first wave – the sounds of combat replaced the sounds of festival.

Downtown Saigon on the eve of the decisive Tet Offensive.

TET SAIGON

ASSAULTS ON THE URBAN CENTER

The Communist plan sent 35 battalions against six primary targets in the Saigon area. Their objectives were the headquarters of the South Vietnamese Joint General Staff (JGS); the Independence Palace, which served as President Thieu's office; the American Embassy; Tan Son Nhut Air Base; the Vietnamese Navy headquarters; and the National Broadcasting Station. Eleven battalions, comprising about 4,000 mostly local men and women, assaulted the city's urban center. The C10 Saigon Sapper Battalion, numbering about 250 men and women who were very familiar with Saigon – many worked as *cyclopousse* or taxicab drivers – spearheaded the attacks. They were to hold the objectives until additional local force battalions arrived to reinforce them.

Shortly before 3am, the guard outside the government radio station saw a small convoy stop and disgorge a group of armed men dressed in South Vietnamese Riot Police uniforms. An officer briskly approached him and announced the reinforcements had arrived. The guard responded: "I haven't heard anything about it." Then the officer shot him.

Years earlier, Viet Cong agents had purchased a house 200 yards from the radio station. There they had stockpiled arms and ammunition for future operations. When the soldiers. assigned to attack the radio station broke out the stored weapons they found termites had eaten through the wooden gun-stocks. Undeterred, they improvised by wrapping rags around the weapons and proceeded with the mission. The well-organized attackers broke into the station while a machine-gunner provided covering fire from a nearby apartment building. His accurate first sweep killed most of the platoon of ARVN paratroopers who lay sleeping on the roof. A North Vietnamese radio specialist followed the assault wave into the station. His job was to play a pre-recorded tape of Ho Chi Minh announcing the liberation of Saigon and the beginning of the General Uprising. He had detailed diagrams of the station layout and duplicate keys provided by an agent on the station's staff.

The foresight of the ARVN lieutenant colonel in charge of the station thwarted these plans. The

A wounded VC fighter and a female nurse captured by ARVN rangers in Saigon during the "Mini-Tet" attacks in the summer of 1968. Similar civilian-clad local VC spearheaded the attacks at Tet.

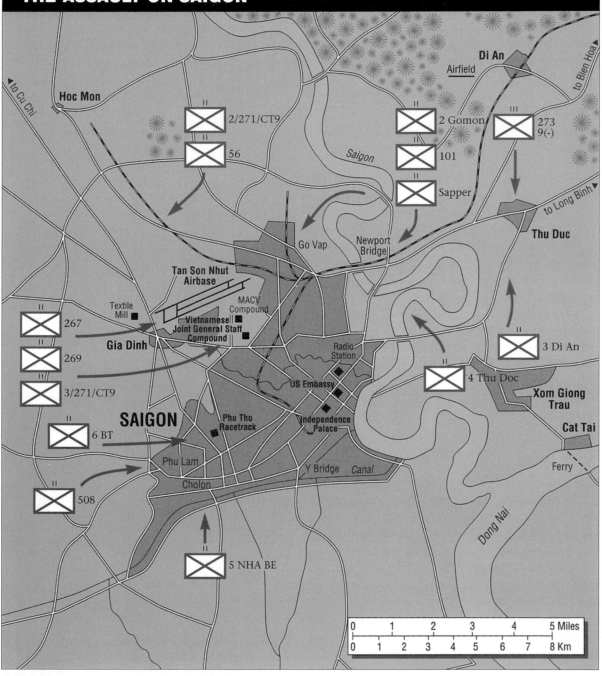

previous afternoon this officer had arranged to take the station off the air if an attack came. Upon hearing gunshots, a technician sent the coded signal and power to the station was cut off. The attackers held their objective for six hours, but were unable to broadcast Ho's message.

The 34 sappers assigned the Independence Palace employed the same commando-style tactics as would be used against the American Embassy. At 1:30am a B-40 rocket exploded on the staff entrance gate. The sappers rushed toward the objective. However, the Palace was one of

the best defended sites in all of South Vietnam. The Palace security force, comprising the presidential guard, national and military police and two tanks, were far too strong for the attackers. Repulsed, they retreated into a nearby building. Such was their discipline that they held out for two days in a futile last-ditch stand. Thirty-two died during this operation.

Against Navy headquarters the Communist high command had devised a complicated plan intended to capture both headquarters and nearby docked ships. The ships would then be used to transport people

Soldiers of the 716th Military Police Battalion across the street from the still-occupied American Embassy.

The damaged side entrance to the embassy and the symbol of tattered American prestige.

from rural areas to Saigon to participate in the General Uprising. In pursuit of this ambitious scheme, twelve sappers blew a hole in the security wall but were unable to make more than a brief penetration. Within five minutes, ten were dead. Here, as often the case nationwide, the attackers had been told to seize the objective and hold until reinforcements arrived. Also, as frequently proved the case, the reinforcements did not exist.

The attack against the JGS compound began at 2:00am. Just as the sappers began their assault on Gate Number 5, an American Military Police patrol jeep appeared. The attackers engaged the jeep, and this pause allowed the ARVN guard to close the gate and prepare a defense. Additional American MPs assisted the defenders and the first assault collapsed. The Communists intended a local force unit, the 2nd (Go Mon) Battalion, to attack Gate Number 4 at the same time, but the assault units were delayed during the approach march. They were not in position until 7:00am. Amazingly, against a thoroughly alert defense they managed to penetrate the JGS compound. But these attackers made the same mistake committed by the sappers who assaulted the American Embassy. Instead of capitalizing on their success – which in this case meant overrunning the virtually undefended nerve center of the entire South Vietnamese military – they dug in and awaited reinforcements. As prisoners later revealed,

EMBASSY ATTACK, SAIGON

2:47am January 31, 1968. Viet Cong guerrillas launch an assault on the United States Embassy Compound.

At a rundown automobile repair shop five blocks from the American Embassy, 19 sappers belonging to the C-10 Battalion boarded a small Peugeot truck and a taxicab to begin the short drive to their objective. A South Vietnamese policeman spotted the vehicles moving without

CHANCERY BUILDING

Lobby: two MPs holed up

Vietnamese Police post (abandoned)

Two-man MP jeep patrol reacting to attack

Main gate

THONG NHUT BOULEVARD

VC truck and taxicab

lights. He chose to avoid trouble and so did nothing. The vehicles turned onto Thong Nhut Boulevard where they encountered the embassy's outer layer of protection provided by four more South Vietnamese police. They too fled without firing a weapon. The vehicles proceeded along the second line of defense, an eight-foot high wall that surrounded the embassy compound. Approaching the night gate, they encountered two American MPs. Although attacks had been taking place throughout Saigon for more than an hour, such was the state of inter-allied communication that the embassy defenders had no idea the Communists had broken the truce. Amid an exchange of gunfire, the MPs backed into the compound and shut the steel gate, thus sealing the embassy from the outside world. At 2:47am a guard radioed the signal that the embassy was under attack.

Meanwhile, out in the street, the

attackers unloaded weapons and explosives. One VC used a satchel charge to blow a three-foot hole in the wall. Displaying formidable courage but poor tactics, both VC officers led the way through the breach. The explosion had alerted the two guards. They whirled around and shot down the officers. One shouted into his radio: "They're coming in! They're coming in! Help me! Help me!" It was his last message. With their burst of accurate fire the two MPs had eliminated the enemy leadership; but they too soon died in the return fire.

A two-man MP jeep patrol responded to the alert and rushed towards the embassy. They also died in a hail of fire from the Viet Cong who remained

outside the wall. Meanwhile two more guards within the embassy itself locked the building's heavy teak doors. Seconds later a rocket grenade smashed through the granite slab on which hung the United States Seal. Its explosion badly wounded one guard. Two more rockets exploded in the lobby followed by a fragmentation grenade. Armed with a .38 pistol, 12-gauge shotgun, and a submachine-gun, the remaining guard resolved to sell himself dearly as he awaited the final VC rush. The only other guard in the embassy tried to

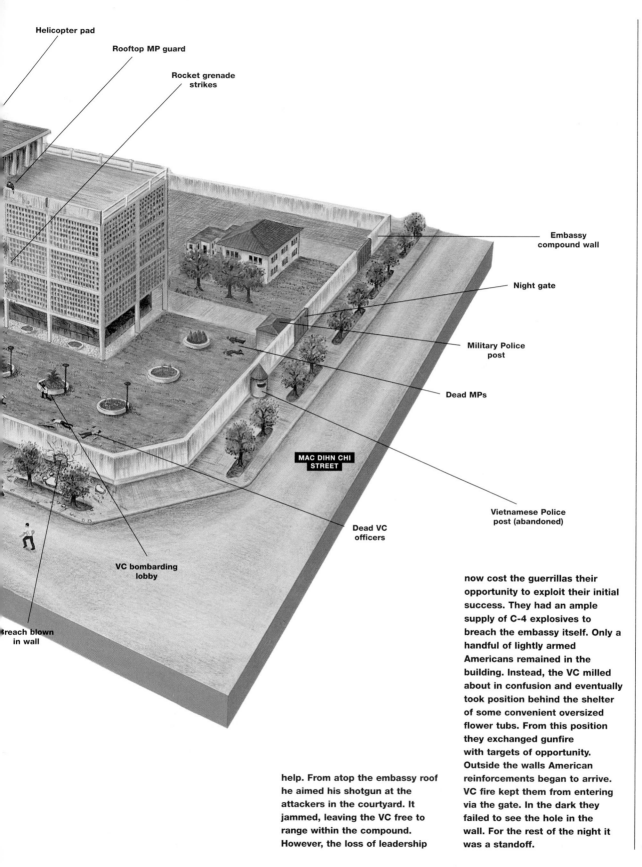

Helicopter pad

Rooftop MP guard

Rocket grenade
strikes

Embassy
compound wall

Night gate

Military Police
post

Dead MPs

Vietnamese Police
post (abandoned)

MAC DIHN CHI
STREET

Dead VC
officers

VC bombarding
lobby

Breach blown
in wall

now cost the guerrillas their opportunity to exploit their initial success. They had an ample supply of C-4 explosives to breach the embassy itself. Only a handful of lightly armed Americans remained in the building. Instead, the VC milled about in confusion and eventually took position behind the shelter of some convenient oversized flower tubs. From this position they exchanged gunfire with targets of opportunity. Outside the walls American reinforcements began to arrive. VC fire kept them from entering via the gate. In the dark they failed to see the hole in the wall. For the rest of the night it was a standoff.

help. From atop the embassy roof he aimed his shotgun at the attackers in the courtyard. It jammed, leaving the VC free to range within the compound. However, the loss of leadership the attackers blindly adhered to the pre-battle plan and thought they had accomplished their mission when they seized a building clearly marked "General Headquarters." In fact, this building was only one of several command buildings, and not the most important.

The failure of initiative allowed an American helicopter to deliver President Thieu to the compound at about noon. Thieu used the command facility as an emergency headquarters. He bravely conducted meetings even while fighting raged about half a mile away. Eventually ARVN airborne and marine units rooted the Go Mon battalion out of the JGS compound. The attackers had come very close to achieving a striking success.

The South Vietnamese had always been sensitive about an American presence in the cities. Bowing to these sensitivities, as a gesture of confidence in ARVN competence, and because of a belief that the Communist threat had diminished, in mid-December the US Command had yielded to the ARVN full responsibility for the close-in defense of Saigon. Thus, only the 1,000-man strong 716th US Army Military Police Battalion (MP) guarded more than 130 American installations in the greater Saigon area. In spite of the alert, only some one-third were at their posts when the VC struck. A mere 25 of the 300 Vietnamese MPs were on hand to assist them.

The 716th MP Battalion's Message Log for the first two hours of the offensive described the widespread, surprise VC attacks:

0300: BOQ No. 3 reports enemy action
0315: US Embassy under attack
0316: Explosion at Phoenix City BOQ
0317: Explosion at Townhouse BOQ
0318: BOQ No. 1 under attack
0319: McArthur BOQ under attack
0321: Report of hostile attack at Rex BOQ
0325: Explosion at BOQ No. 2
0340: Automatic-weapons fire and attack at BOQ No. 3
0341: MPs at US Embassy request urgent ammo resupply
0342: Heavy sniper fire at Metropole BEQ
0350: Incoming mortars at Montana BEQ
0358: Saigon port area reports small-arms and automatic-weapons fire
0359: Mortars and rockets fired at US Embassy; reinforcements
        requested
0407: MP jeep C9A reports that 2-ton truck carrying 25-man reaction
        team to BOQ No.3 hit by rockets and claymore mines. Heavy
        casualties
0408: Jeep C9A hit; both MPs killed
0419: BOQ No. 3 pleads for ammo resupply
0420: General Westmoreland calls; orders first priority effort to
        recapture US Embassy
0430: Request armored vehicles and helicopters for embassy assault
0449: Cleveland and Columbia BOQ request ammo and assistance
0550: Three claymores detonated at Saigon motor pool. Booby traps
        discovered.

Shortly after the first alert, the commander of the 716th implemented the "disaster plan." Designed for such emergencies as riots or isolated bombings, it was woefully inappropriate for the chaos of

Combat sequence at Bachelor
Officer Quarters No. 3:
ABOVE **During the night the first
reinforcements arrived via truck,
hit a claymore mine, and
suffered heavy losses.**
RIGHT **Reserves, following an
ARVN V-100 armored car, tried to
work up the alley to rescue the
wounded at the truck. Heavy fire
drove off the armored car.**
(continued on page 50)

combat sweeping through Saigon. Jeeps and open-topped trucks, such as
those mentioned in the 0407 and 0408 entries above, rushed to respond
to the dozens of emergencies. Their bravery mattered less than their lack
of firepower and training. By dawn the VC had made major penetrations

Combat sequence at Bachelor Officer Quarters No. 3 (continued from page 49):
TOP LEFT **More South Vietnamese and US reinforcements arrived to resume the advance.**
BOTTOM LEFT **MPs pinned down by heavy VC fire.**
TOP RIGHT **Resistance finally crumbled and VC suspects were removed.**
BOTTOM RIGHT **Allied casualties from the fighting. Sixteen MPs died and 21 were wounded in the fighting around BOQ No. 3.**

into western and southern Saigon and controlled large areas in the suburb of Cholon. The widespread attacks such as those described in the 716th's Message Log typically featured a handful of attackers. However, initial reports could not assess the size of the enemy forces. To the American officer commanding the Saigon area, General Weyand, it was difficult to make sense of the multiple enemy thrusts. The fact his own headquarters was under rocket and ground attack also hampered tactical judgment. The map showing the reported attacks around Saigon reminded him of "a pinball machine, one light after another going on as it was hit." Between 3am and 5am he shifted some 5,000 mechanized and airborne troops to defend the various installations under assault. His rapid, yet considered reactions limited enemy success.

CAVALRY TO THE RESCUE

Fifteen miles north of Saigon was the Long Binh logistical and command complex. This sprawling base area, which extended to the enormous Bien Hoa Air Base, was a target too big to overlook by Communist planners. At 3:00am an intense rocket and mortar barrage pelted the area. The veteran 275th VC Regiment assaulted Long Binh's northern perimeter while a local VC battalion launched a diversionary attack against the eastern bunker line. Meanwhile VC sappers infiltrated the huge ammunition dump just north of Long Binh. Simultaneously, the 274th VC Regiment attacked Bien Hoa.

While well coordinated and bravely driven home, these attacks fell victim to superb American mobility and firepower. Half an hour after the opening barrage, the 2/47th Battalion (mechanized) began a speed march from Bear Cat toward Long Binh. At first light the 2nd Battalion/560th Infantry airlifted into Bien Hoa Air Base. The élite 11th Armored Cavalry Regiment, the Blackhorse Regiment, made a twelve-hour forced march to arrive at Long Binh during the day. Once in position, the multiple machine-guns of the mechanized units' APCs shot apart all Viet Cong attacks. Perhaps above them all was the performance of the mechanized cavalry troop of the 9th Infantry Division.

At bases northeast of Saigon, the radio net of 1/5 Armored Cavalry, 9th Infantry Division, came alive at 6am on January 31. The squadron learned that large enemy forces were attacking Tan Son Nhut, Bien Hoa, Long Binh, and Saigon itself. Officers paid particular attention to news from Long Binh, where one of the Division's mechanized battalions had been sent the night before. By listening to that battalion's tactical radios, the squadron anticipated that soon it would be needed. One hour later came the order for Troop A to move out.

RIGHT **Descended from Second World War tanks, the M-48 medium tank served as the mainstay of the American armor during the Vietnam War. A crew of four, comprising a commander, gunner, loader, and driver manned the tank. Its armament consisted of a 90mm gun, a 7.62mm machine-gun by the commander's cupola, and a .50cal machine-gun by the loader's cupola. With a top speed of 30mph, it had surprising "jungle busting" cross-country ability. Although heavily armored, tanks sacrificed their mobility and thus proved vulnerable in urban combat. A Patton belonging to the 11th Armored Cavalry supports operations on February 2 around Bien Hoa.**

Soldiers of the 2/47th Battalion (mechanized) assault VC positions in the Long Binh area.

Amid great confusion, the squadron commander ordered the troop, minus one-third of its strength left behind to garrison a fire-support base, to begin a speed march to Bien Hoa. Hardly had the troop left its base than it ran into an ambush. The VC had skillfully anticipated American reactions, but they underestimated the cavalry's mobility and firepower. The troop drove through the ambush while laying down a carpet of fire from their ACAVs. Without suffering serious damage, Troop A cleared

Some of the VC killed by the APCs of the 9th Infantry Division.

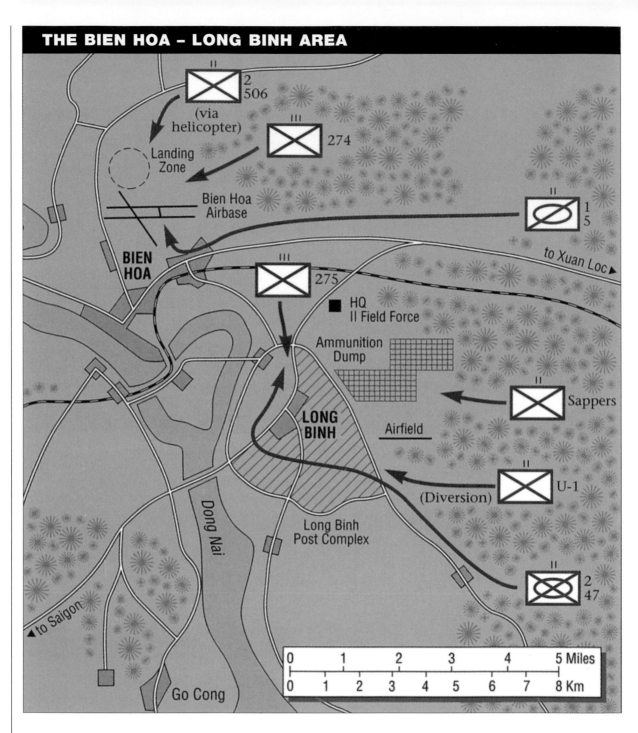

the fire zone only to encounter a mile-long strip of houses each one of which seemed to conceal an enemy gunner. Beginning to take losses, the troop managed to speed through the gauntlet.

The column's lead tank came to a small concrete bridge and rolled across it without incident. Suddenly an explosion rocked the air and the bridge collapsed in fragments. The troop's ACAVs managed to ford the stream, but the balance of the heavier tanks had to remain behind. Troop A entered the city of Bien Hoa where it found the central square

**M35A2 "gun truck" of
27th Transportation Battalion.
Illustration by Peter Sarson
and Tony Bryan.**

crowded with people. It pushed through the throng, but suddenly the troopers realized that the "crowd" was actually several companies of enemy soldiers. The enemy simultaneously realized that they confronted American armor. The Viet Cong's initial volleys disabled two ACAVs. More ACAVs entered the square and opened fire with all their weapons. They drove the VC to cover, pushed the knocked-out vehicles aside, rescued their crews, and pressed on for the airbase. The column now comprised one tank and eight ACAVs.

The reassuring words of the squadron commander filled the radio. From an overhead helicopter he directed the cavalry through the byzantine labyrinth of narrow streets. Nearing the air base he spotted hundreds of enemy soldiers belonging to the 274th VC Regiment lining Highway 1, apparently deployed to stop any relieving column. His warning saved the column. Exploiting its mobility, the cavalry left the highway and drove a parallel route. The ACAVs' machine-guns shot up the unsuspecting enemy from the rear and finally reached the beleaguered air base.

Its presence at Bien Hoa provided the narrow margin between victory and defeat. Along with the 2nd Battalion/506th Infantry, it repulsed all assaults. By day's end its one tank had been hit nineteen times and the crew replaced twice. Of the twelve ACAVs that began the mission, only six still ran by nightfall. The troop had suffered heavily, but the survivors felt elation that after months of being the target of ambushes without being able to hit back, it had finally met a stand-up enemy and inflicted terrible losses upon him.

A cavalry officer describes his unit's feelings on the first day of February:

"I can still remember the feeling of pride we had in our operations center the next morning when we heard the squadron commander's initial report … that Saigon, Bien Hoa, and Long Binh were literally ringed in steel … Five cavalry squadrons had moved through the previous day and night, converging on the Saigon area. When dawn broke, they formed an almost-continuous chain of more than five hundred fighting vehicles … We actually cheered … from that morning the outcome was never in doubt. We knew that our enemy could never match our mobility, flexibility, and firepower."

THE PRESS REACTION

Within fifteen minutes of the first attack, an Associated Press (AP) reporter had typed out the first bulletin announcing the attack. By a twist of fate that was to have immense consequences, the embassy was close to the quarters housing the Western Press. This allowed reporters to rush to the scene of the action. The resultant concentration of the Press undoubtedly distorted the significance of the combat. Because they could not see over the walls, neither they nor the soldiers knew what was going on inside. Consequently they relied upon the excited comments of one of the MPs who was outside the walls. This MP stated: "They're in the embassy." When a reporter asked an MP captain for confirmation, he replied: "My God, yes … we are taking fire from up there … keep your head down." This information was sufficient for AP to send a bulletin stating:

"The Vietcong seized part of the US Embassy in Saigon early Wednesday … Communist commandos penetrated the supposedly attack-proof building in the climax of a combined artillery and guerrilla assault that brought limited warfare to Saigon itself."

A dead VC next to a landscape planter inside the embassy compound. His rocket launcher and equipment lie nearby.

This bulletin arrived just before the first-edition deadlines for very influential morning newspapers in the eastern USA. Headline writers quickly updated their papers and spread the shocking message that the enemy had captured the symbol of American prestige.

In Saigon, the American command failed to appreciate the importance of the embassy combat. The commander on the spot was quite content to wait for daylight before proceeding. He knew he had the VC cornered. At higher command levels the numerous actions exploding all over the country seemed to demand more attention. Responding to pressure from Washington, around 5am Westmoreland had Weyand send a helicopter with a platoon of airborne soldiers to land on the embassy roof. Automatic weapons fire from the surviving VC drove it off. To avoid unnecessary risks, the higher command decided to wait for daylight before trying again. By the time the helicopter returned, MPs had forced the embassy gate. They easily killed the few surviving VC. What an American participant called "a piddling platoon action" was over after a six hour combat.

Reporters swarmed the grounds as military spokesmen tried to explain what had happened. Controversy centered on whether the VC had actually entered the embassy. Although they had not technically entered the embassy building, the AP stood by their opposing claim. Too often reporters had been deceived by official pronouncements. AP's insistence that the VC had entered the embassy further undercut the credibility of official statements and set the stage for one of the most memorable visual images in this, the world's first television war.

At 9:20am, Westmoreland arrived at the just-secured compound dressed in an immaculately pressed and starched uniform and held a hastily arranged Press conference. In America viewers saw a scene of carnage. Dead VC sappers littered the embassy grounds, their bodies sprawled around the flower pots. Blood, death, and battle damage abounded. In the midst of an embassy apparently under siege, the general explained that the enemy never penetrated the embassy itself. He exuded confidence and claimed the allies were returning to the offensive.

A *Washington Post* reporter recalls: "The reporters could hardly believe their ears. Westmoreland was standing in the ruins and saying everything was great." An AP reporter later explained that, given the record over the years, "we had little faith in what General Westmoreland stated." When the American public read their morning papers they received two impressions: the Viet Cong had seized the embassy itself; and Westmoreland was lying when he said they had not. The psychological damage done to the American war effort would become clearer in the coming weeks.

THE PHU THO RACETRACK

In spite of complete surprise and the initial success of many of the opening assaults, on the Communist side events were not proceeding as desired. There was no general uprising and little active civilian support in Saigon. In order to preserve secrecy, the VC units that attacked Saigon had little knowledge of the overall picture. Most had received the briefing that they were to take part in an attack of unspecified dimensions. However necessary for security reasons, this secrecy prevented all unit coordination. Thus, while achieving numerous isolated initial successes, once in position the VC had to fend for themselves against a growing Allied counterattack.

Repulsed or evicted from their six prime objectives, the attackers broke down into small units and took shelter in buildings throughout Saigon. In particular, the attackers clung to the Phu Tho racetrack area.

A burned out M-113 on the Phu Tho racetrack. The APC was hit by VC rocket fire.

The 6th BT VC Battalion had seized the racetrack during its opening assault. Communist planners valued this objective because it was the hub of several major roads, possession of its open terrain denied the Allies a potential landing zone for helicopters bringing reinforcements, and it provided an easily recognized rallying place for rural VC unfamiliar with Saigon.

The first warning of the enemy build-up in the Phu Tho area came at 4:45am when a 716th MP jeep patrol radioed: "The driver caught a slug in the gut and I'm under heavy automatic weapons fire. Can you give me some help?" Then the radio went dead. Before help arrived the two MPs had been killed.

A company from the 199th Infantry Brigade (Light) boarded trucks and APCs and headed for the racetrack at 8:00am on January 31. Six blocks from the objective it met heavy automatic weapons fire from rooftops and buildings lining the road. A VC rocket struck the lead APC killing the platoon leader and two crew. VC rifle, machine-gun, and grenade fire hammered the column as it slowly advanced towards the racetrack. When heavy enemy fire repulsed its first charge, the infantry regrouped and tried again. Supported by helicopter gunships and recoilless rifle fire, they captured the racetrack by 4:30pm. At dusk a reinforcing company landed on the racetrack itself and the Americans prepared a defensive perimeter.

Over the next several days additional reinforcements arrived, including the 33rd ARVN Ranger Battalion, and together the Allies expanded their control to the areas adjacent to Phu Tho. It was not easy. An American mechanized company, driving through a narrow street three blocks away, suddenly was hit by a VC rocket and machine-gun ambush. The opening barrage destroyed the two rearmost APCs and heavily damaged a third. However, its crew stood by their guns to provide covering fire while the accompanying infantry dragged the dead and wounded clear of the kill zone. Then the survivors hustled back to the racetrack itself just in time to help repulse a large-scale VC counterattack. The fighting ebbed and flowed around Phu Tho for several more days. Eventually, every Viet Cong unit that participated in the Saigon offensive contributed manpower to this battle.

As early as February 1, COSVN, the Communist high command, realized that many elements of its grand plan had miscarried. While complimenting its soldiers for their performance, it sent out orders that

called off further assaults against fortified Allied positions. Furthermore, it criticized faulty coordination and liaison and noted serious tactical shortcomings. None the less, not until March 7, five weeks after the first attack, did ARVN Rangers finally clear the entire capital city of Saigon.

As late as February 10, US reinforcements, including these soldiers of the 199th Light Infantry Brigade, were still reinforcing the Phu Tho position. The trucks are parked on the running surface.

Dead Viet Cong on perimeter of Tan Son Nhut Air Base, February 1.

TET COUNTRYWIDE

SURPRISE AT DA NANG

While the Saigon and Hue battles monopolized most attention from Allied commanders and the Press, fierce Communist assaults took place all over South Vietnam. Here ARVN and militia forces bore the brunt of the ground defense. Part of the ferocity derived from the briefings given to many of the assault troops. They were told that they were engaged in an offensive that was to lead to a general uprising. In keeping with this brave talk, about half the assault units did not receive any instructions regarding a withdrawal in the event of unforeseen circumstances.

While South Vietnamese authorities failed to disseminate word of the canceled truce in Saigon, in the smaller provincial and district towns some units were on full alert. This made a great difference when the Communists struck. After the event, high-ranking South Vietnamese and American officers would claim that official policy called for holiday leaves for only ten percent of all manpower. In fact, a much more liberal policy was in effect. Typical was the 7th ARVN Division, which had 4,000 men present and 3,500 on leave when the attack came.

The first assault wave utilized local VC units, sappers, and in-place agents. The Communist attacks strove to disrupt further South Vietnamese improvements by targeting headquarters, training and logistical bases. Every attack also featured an assault against the local radio station. Just as in Saigon, the attackers carried tapes to broadcast in hopes of stirring up the popular uprising. In general, the attacks' success depended upon two conditions: were the defenders alerted with leaves canceled and in position; were the Americans able to bring their heavy firepower to bear even at the risk of civilian losses?

The abortive assault on Da Nang, the country's second largest city, demonstrated this point. A police agent who had infiltrated the local VC organization warned of the coming blow. None the less, a reinforced company briefly penetrated the headquarters of the South Vietnamese I Corps on the city outskirts. When the dashing corps commander, Lieutenant General Hoang Xuan Lam, first heard from a staff officer that an assault was under way he responded incredulously: "Baloney, baloney!" Assured that it was true, he drove through enemy fire to reach his headquarters at dawn. Assessing the situation, Lam tapped the map with his swagger stick and spoke to his U.S. adviser, Major P.S. Milantoni:

"Milantoni, bomb here. Use big bombs."

"General, that's pretty close."

"Bomb."

The adviser requested the mission only to be told by another American officer that the mission was so close to friendly positions that it would never get clearance. Milantoni replied: "General Lam just gave it." The bombs struck a mere 200 yards from I Corps headquarters. The VC fire diminished and Lam ordered more strikes. When the VC pulled back, the South Vietnamese general sent helicopter gunships in pursuit. The VC attack on Da Nang failed.

BATTLE IN THE DELTA

The Mobile Riverine Force (MRF) was a special American brigade-sized outfit equipped for the unique combat conditions in the Mekong Delta. It moved through the myriad rivers and canals aboard assault boats and possessed numerous improvised weapons such as 60-foot long monitors armed with a revolving armored turret housing a 40mm cannon intended for close fire support. It had specially designed floating artillery barges to provide heavier firepower. All of these weapons and more were attempts to solve the constant problem of the Vietnam War, how to find and fight an elusive enemy who usually revealed himself only when his first shots announced an ambush. When the Tet Offensive exploded in the Delta, the problem was not locating the enemy. The Viet Cong seemed to be everywhere.

In the Mekong Delta, the Communists assaulted thirteen of sixteen provincial cities. Such was the ferocity of their attacks that Allied intelligence soon identified all except one battalion listed on its order of battle. In other words, the Communists were sending in all their men. Furthermore, captured plans revealed a notable absence of the customary contingency plans for retreat. Apparently the attackers planned to hold their ground. The MRF, on the other hand, manned dispersed positions along waterways in an effort to interdict VC supply

Few American units operated in the heavily populated Delta region south of Saigon. The notable exception was the joint Army/Navy Mobile Riverine Force (MRF). Built around two brigades of the 9th Infantry Division, the MRF had unique assets suitable for the labyrinth of rivers, canals and rice paddies characteristic of the Delta. In most of Vietnam, the Allies used helicopters to reach the enemy in otherwise inaccessible terrain. In the waterlogged Delta, the Allies employed specially designed watercraft. They included armored troop carriers known as Tango boats after their call sign. The Tango boat featured stand-off armor designed to detonate RPG or recoilless rocket rounds before they hit the boat's armor. Used as assault craft, the Tango boats glided through the shallows to land infantry on dikes and levees.

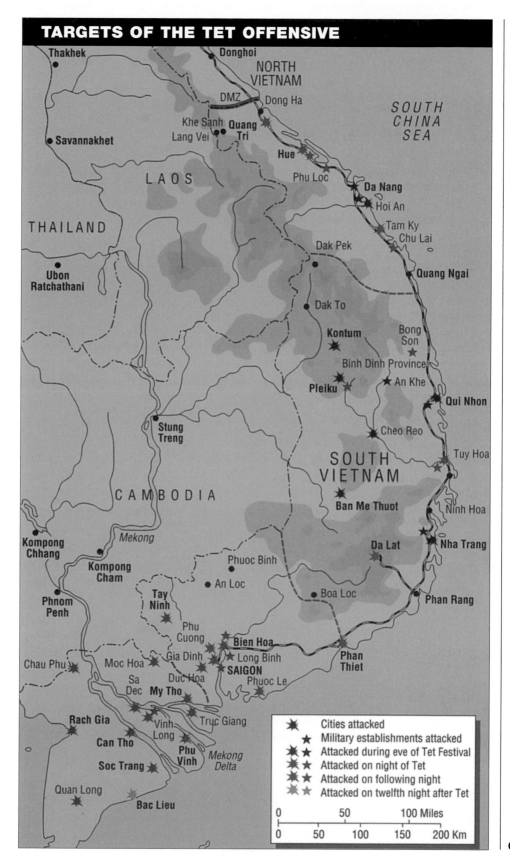

TARGETS OF THE TET OFFENSIVE

Thakhek

Donghoi

NORTH
VIETNAM

DMZ · Dong Ha

Khe Sanh Quang
Lang Vei Tri

Savannakhet

SOUTH
CHINA
SEA

Hue

LAOS

Phu Loc

Da Nang
Hoi An

THAILAND

Tam Ky
Chu Lai

Dak Pek

Ubon
Ratchathani

Quang Ngai

Dak To

Bong
Son

Kontum

Binh Dinh Province

An Khe

Pleiku

Qui Nhon

Stung
Treng

Cheo Reo

SOUTH
VIETNAM

Tuy Hoa

Ban Me Thuot

Ninh Hoa

CAMBODIA

Kompong
Chhang

Mekong

Da Lat

Nha Trang

Kompong
Cham

Phuoc Binh

Boa Loc

Phan Rang

Phnom
Penh

An Loc

Tay
Ninh

Phu
Cuong

Bien Hoa

Chau Phu

Moc Hoa

Gia Dinh

Long Binh

Phan
Thiet

Sa
Dec

Duc Hoa

SAIGON

My Tho

Phuoc Le

Rach Gia

Truc Giang

Vinh
Long

Can Tho

Phu
Vinh

Mekong
Delta

Soc Trang

Quan Long

Bac Lieu

✸		Cities attacked
	★	Military establishments attacked
✸	★	Attacked during eve of Tet Festival
✸	★	Attacked on night of Tet
✸	★	Attacked on following night
✸	★	Attacked on twelfth night after Tet

0   50   100 Miles

0   50   100   150   200 Km

63

lines. Units had to concentrate hastily before counterattacking VC penetrations in various urban settings.

Their first call was to My Tho, south of Saigon. Three VC battalions and a sapper company had entered the city while one battalion remained on the outskirts. Two MRF battalions hastened to the city to support the units of the embattled 7th ARVN Division. It took three days to recapture My Tho. The battle featured tough house-to-house fighting, a type of combat very different from the MRF's normal mission and one unsuited to its special weaponry. Like a fire brigade, once it had secured My Tho, MRF units rushed to other threatened positions including Saigon itself.

For an unprecedented thirty consecutive days the Mobile Riverine Force fought without rest. Its contributions were key to the many tactical

A scout dog team belonging to the 4th Infantry Division flushes out enemy snipers still clinging to Kontum five days after the Communists attacked the city.

successes gained in the Delta. General Westmoreland, taking a typical American view that undervalued ARVN fighting, said afterwards: "The MRF saved the Delta." Indeed, its stout fighting justified the Presidential Unit Citation it earned. Still, here as elsewhere, tactical success could not conceal the hard truth that the Viet Cong had demonstrated to the civilian population of the Delta that, despite American support, they

In the war against the French, the Vietminh had successfully recruited sympathizers by entering urban areas and forcing the French to employ heavy weapons to drive them out. They then blamed the civilian losses on the French. By occupying churches, pagodas, schools, and hospitals, the Communists created the same dilemma for the Americans during the 1968 Tet Offensive. Vietnamese civilians return to their destroyed homes near Bien Hoa on February 2.

could strike anywhere, anytime. Since ultimately the war would have to be won or lost through the effort of the South Vietnamese, this demonstration contributed to Communist strategic victory.

An MRF boat captain well understood the consequences of the Tet Offensive in the Delta: "After Tet this whole country really changed." Speaking of a town badly damaged in the fighting, he continued: "The VC really tore the place up and I think the Americans more or less got blamed for it. We had to evacuate the town and when we did go back … there were quite a few Vietnamese people around who kind of looked down on us a little for leaving them." Supporting this captain's analysis was the experience of the Mekong Delta river city of Ben Tre, which was home to some 35,000 civilians. A reinforced VC regiment numbering about 2,500 men attacked and gained substantial footholds within the city. To evict the Viet Cong, the Allies had to summon artillery and air strikes. This caused extensive damage to the city and produced one of the most memorable quotes of the war. While explaining what had taken place to a reporter, an American major said: "It became necessary to destroy the town to save it." The American Press played this quote to the hilt, using it to epitomize the seeming futility of the war effort.

THE CENTRAL HIGHLANDS

Fierce fighting also took place in the twelve central provinces. Major ground attacks struck seven provincial capitals and three other objectives. At Qui Nhon, a coastal city in II Corps area, before the attacks began, the ARVN defenders discovered the Communist plan when they captured eleven VC agents. But such was the muddle within South Vietnamese units at Tet that Communist sappers assaulted exactly as revealed and still seized their objectives. The attackers even seized the

Captured .50cal machine-gun and Soviet-made rocket launcher mounted on stand. In background are two captured flags.

jail, where they captured the ARVN captain who had directed the successful raid that had bagged the eleven agents.

Typical was the battle of Ban Me Thuot in the Central Highlands. Here the 23rd ARVN Division had captured a plan for an attack on the city on about January 20. The divisional commander, Colonel Dao Quang An, accordingly canceled his unit's Tet leave. He put out patrols six miles from the city, and these patrols ambushed elements of the 33rd NVA Regiment as they were moving into position. None the less, the fighting at Ban Me Thuot raged for three and a half days, with the ARVN soldiers taking heavy losses because of their inexperience in city fighting. Reluctantly, An decided he had to employ artillery and air strikes despite the resultant civilian devastation. Yet the battle continued for a solid nine days, the city center changing hands four times before the 23rd ARVN Division regained control. An's leadership greatly impressed the Americans. An adviser commented that had he not decided to cancel Tet leaves and to deploy far-ranging ambush patrols, the city would have fallen. Further, the adviser told MACV that An's tactical handling of the battle had been flawless.

In sharp contrast was the conduct of the major general commanding in the delta. When the attack struck he was at his fortified headquarters protected by tanks and armored infantry. He did not emerge for days, leaving his American advisers to conduct the defense. Similarly, the ARVN colonel commanding at Vinh Long cracked under the strain of events. When an American officer reported helicopters receiving fire and asked permission to return fire, all he received was a blank stare. Another adviser found the province chief wearing civilian clothes under his military uniform – just in case.

Despite heavy fighting in many places, Allied units regained control in most provincial cities within a week. On February 7, NVA tanks spearheaded an assault that overran the Lang Vei Special Forces Camp near Khe Sanh. With hearts in their throats, the American high command wondered if this were the start of the long-expected attack on Khe Sanh. Perhaps it was just another diversionary attack against a convenient and exposed target, because the Communist high command chose not to try to exploit this success. On February 17–18 the Viet Cong created a brief stir when they made artillery assaults against Allied installations

Typical soldier of the North Vietnamese Army. Illustration by Mike Chappell.

throughout the country. But in comparison with the initial operations, these were low effort/low risk harassing affairs. After the first week sustained combat took place only in Saigon and Hue.

By February 21, the VC/NVA high command faced battlefield reality. Their assaults had been extremely costly and had failed to achieve the predicted success. Accordingly, COSVN issued orders for its units still in contact around the cities to retreat. There were to be no more ground assaults on fortified Allied installations. Instead, COSVN ordered units to revert to hit-and-run tactics characterized by mortar and rocket bombardment and sapper raids. COSVN made one exception – the units in Hue were to hold their positions.

BLOODY HUE

he Imperial City of Hue was the most venerated place in Vietnam. The stone walls of its inner citadel had been built with the aid of the French in the 1800s. Peking's Forbidden City had served as the model for Hue's citadel. Thus it was a place full of gardens, moats, and intricate stone buildings. Standing above the citadel was the highest flagpole in South Vietnam, as such, the most visible symbol of the South's struggle for independence. Communist planners did not overlook what was, with the clarity of hindsight, such an obvious target.

Surrounded by rows of thick-walled masonry houses, with many streets too narrow to permit access by Marine armor, the Citadel at Hue was a difficult position to even approach. Tall trees and hedgerows limited visibility to 25 yards. With two weeks to prepare, the defenders dug hundreds of camouflaged, mutually supporting positions rendering the Citadel an extremely tough objective. The old fortress and flag tower, from where the Communist banner flew during the long battle.

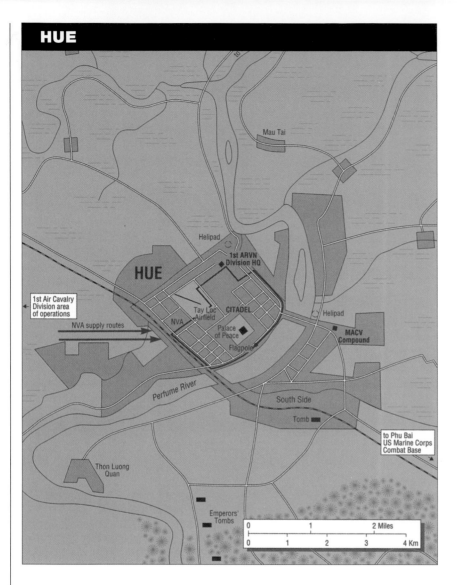

The war had not touched Hue, yet it was more than a symbolic target. A rail and highway bridge crossed the Perfume River and continued north. They served as the main land supply routes for the growing number of Allied troops along the DMZ. Hue also served as a major unloading point for waterborne supplies that were brought from Da Nang on the coast.

The attackers possessed very detailed information about Hue. They had divided the Right Bank into four tactical areas and had pinpointed nearly every civil and military installation. Viet Cong intelligence officers had prepared a priority list of 196 targets and had listed individuals to be captured. The plan called for their evacuation if possible; otherwise they were to be killed. In addition, "Cruel tyrants and reactionary elements" – categories encompassing most South Vietnamese officials, military officers, politicians, Americans and foreigners except the French – were to be separated, taken outside the city and "punished" – meaning killed. The Viet Cong carefully laid the groundwork for what became their most horrific atrocity.

On January 30, a US Army radio intercept unit overheard Communist orders calling for an attack on Hue that night. Following standard procedure, it forwarded the message through channels. The Hue defenders did not receive the message in time. It was another in a long list of intelligence failures relating to the Tet Offensive.

Inside the city, Brigadier General Ngo Quang Truong, the commander of the 1st ARVN Division, had received Westmoreland's alert calling for cancellation of the cease-fire. Considered one of the best South Vietnamese generals, Truong gathered his staff at his HQ compound and kept them on 100 percent alert. This vigilance paid dividends when the enemy attack struck. But over half his division's manpower still received holiday leave. Furthermore, given Hue's record as an "open" city, Truong did not think the Communists would attack the city itself. He positioned his battalions to defend outside the urban area. Here too was a failure in preparation.

When the attack came, the only regular garrison comprised the all-volunteer Hoc Bao (Black Panther) Reconnaissance Company, 1st ARVN Division. They guarded Truong's HQ in the northern corner of the citadel. Scattered throughout the rest of the city were support troops. Across the Perfume River was the South Side, where a Military Assistance Command Vietnam (MACV) compound housed American and Australian advisers and staff. These two strongpoints were to become islands of resistance when the 12th VC and Hue City VC Sapper Battalions, two NVA infantry regiments, and a rocket battalion flooded the city.

At 2am, January 31, one of Truong's outlying patrols reported at least two enemy battalions advancing on the city. Apparently the Tet-induced torpor prevented him from making much use of this warning. In any

Joining the "A" Company convoy were two Army "Dusters," 40mm antiaircraft weapons used with deadly effect against ground targets.

event, he did not notify his allies at the MACV compound. They first learned of the enemy's presence an hour and forty minutes later when a dozen 122mm rockets detonated in their compound. Additional rocket and mortar bombardment provided preparatory fire while local VC, who had already infiltrated Hue dressed as civilians, took up positions to await the arrival of NVA assault troops hurrying into the city.

The Communists mistimed their first assault on the MACV compound. Instead of following on the heels of the rockets, they waited some five minutes. This gave the defenders just enough time to gather weapons and man defensive positions. A brave army soldier purchased another five minutes by manning an exposed machine-gun position atop a 20-foot wooden tower built on the compound's walls. His fire stopped the first rush of some forty NVA soldiers belonging to the 4th Infantry Regiment, who tried to advance to the walls to set satchel charges. A B-40 rocket round toppled him from his perch and allowed the attackers to storm the gate. Here they encountered some US Marines manning a bunker. They too slowed the attack until falling to a hail of RPG rounds. The time bravely bought allowed the defenders, including a tough crew of Australian warrant officers, to form a cohesive defense. The enemy changed tactics and tried to subdue the garrison with mortars and automatic weapons fire delivered from overlooking buildings. Isolated, unaware that enemy attacks had exploded nation wide, the garrison hunkered down and prayed for help.

All around their compound, and across the river, the 4th and 6th NVA Regiments and their VC comrades controlled most of the city and were freely roaming the streets. While the combat soldiers began fortifying mortar and machine-gun positions, special operatives began

Marine Corps Patton tanks helped the grunts edge their way forward through Hue's streets. An officer recalls that the tanks drew heavy enemy fire: "The moment a tank stuck its nose around the corner of a building, it looked like the Fourth of July" such was the volume and variety of hostile fire. One tank received 121 hits and went through five crews. Survivors came out looking "like they were punch drunk." This Patton halts before a destroyed canal bridge in Hue.

Platoon Sergeant Alfredo Gonzalez, 21 years old, served with Alpha Company during its ambush on January 31. When his unit suffered intense enemy fire, and although wounded from multiple shrapnel hits, Gonzalez rushed through the kill zone to rescue wounded Marines and drag them to shelter. Later in the action, he crawled along a roadside ditch to hand-grenade an enemy machine-gun that continued to pin his unit down. Four days later, having refused medical evacuation, while fighting through the Joan of Arc School, Gonzalez kicked in a door and led the rush into a school room. The NVA fired a hail of RPGs from point-blank range across the courtyard. The sergeant returned the fire with LAW rockets and silenced the enemy position. Suddenly a last enemy rocket entered the room striking Gonzalez in the midsection. Called "the perfect Marine" by his officer, Gonzalez received a posthumous Medal of Honor for his conduct on January 31.

rounding up the people on their numerous lists. From atop the Citadel flagpole, a huge red-blue-gold Viet Cong flag flew. It had taken about two hours for the Communists to capture Hue, the country's second largest city.

RELIEF FORCE

Eight miles south of the city was the US Marine Corps Phu Bai Combat Base. Here the assistant commander of the 1st Marine Division, Brigadier General Foster LaHue, sifted through reports telling him of enemy activity throughout his area of responsibility. Included in the reports was one sent by the beleaguered defenders of the MACV compound, which had slowly drifted through the chain of command. Having been filtered by so many command levels, it conveyed little sense of urgency. Amid the confusion, LaHue apparently failed to appreciate both the scale and the critical nature of events in Hue. But, responding to orders, he did send reinforcements. Two and a half platoons belonging to "A" Company, 1/1 Marines, boarded trucks and headed for Hue, not knowing that close to a full division of enemy soldiers awaited them.

Fortunately, the Marines married up with four M-48 Patton tanks along the way. As the small convoy neared Hue's outskirts, Communist marksmen opened fire and wounded several grunts. The convoy ran the gauntlet of fire, crossed a teetering canal bridge that enemy sappers had partially destroyed, and approached a cluster of buildings. They reminded the company commander, Captain Gordon Batcheller, of an old western town, two-storey wooden buildings with no sidewalks, and – most ominously – with no people. The captain ordered his men out of the trucks and on to the tanks. Then, in best Marine Corps tradition, he boarded the lead tank and ordered the advance. From the tank decks the grunts sprayed the buildings with fire as they drove by. In return came a tremendous volume of AK-47 fire and volleys of RPGs. One RPG thudded into the leading tank spraying Batcheller with shrapnel and cutting the legs off his radioman. The survivors gathered along a ditch and tended their wounded. From adjacent buildings and rooftops Batcheller could see NVA infantrymen firing at his unit. It was very different from the paddy and jungle war where one seldom saw the enemy. Alpha Company needed help.

Around noon the commanders at Phu Bai learned of "A" Company's plight. Lieutenant Colonel Marcus Gravel received the mission of taking another company, Golf 2/5, forward to retrace Alpha Company's steps and try to relieve them. He had no information other than Alpha Company was pinned down. Naked valor would have to substitute for preparation, firepower, and tactics. Although the NVA would ambush, with dismal regularity, most of the convoys that drove along the road to Hue, this group made it without incident. They joined Alpha Company's survivors, now led by a wounded gunnery sergeant, and fought their way towards the MACV compound. A dug-in NVA machine-gun opened fire. Although already wounded, Sergeant Alfredo Gonzalez crawled towards it along a roadside ditch. Drawing near, he tossed a grenade into the position and silenced the machine-gun. The advance continued to the MACV compound. One of the defenders was to recall: "I have little doubt that many of us would not be alive today, had those Marines not arrived."

Once the objective had been attained, helicopters arrived to take out the many wounded. Then Gravel's two much-reduced companies received new orders from LaHue. He was to drive across the Perfume River, through the Citadel, and link up with General Truong in the 1st ARVN Division compound. Gravel protested to no avail. LaHue radioed back: "Proceed." Sadly, headquarters was out of touch with reality and would remain so for far too long. The misguided effort inevitably failed. The advance reached halfway across the Perfume River bridge when NVA machine-gunners opened fire. Ten Marines fell dead or wounded in the opening volley. Golf Company pressed on, only to be ambushed in the narrow, winding streets bordering the Citadel. Gravel ordered an unauthorized retreat. Fifty of Golf's 150 men had been killed or wounded. That night, Gravel raged against the foolish orders that had sent his men to their doom. The only thing he felt thankful for was that the NVA had made a mistake too. Instead of holding fire just a little longer, which would have drawn Golf Company hopelessly into the maze of streets near the Citadel, they had shown their inexperience and fired too soon. The thought that the other side made mistakes provided some

BELOW **A Marine observation plane makes a low-level pass over the Perfume River. Lieutenant Colonel Gravel's Marines successfully assaulted the river but could not expand their bridgehead on the far side.**

ABOVE **M48A3 Patton tank of 1st Tank Battalion, USMC, Hue. Illustration by Peter Sarson and Tony Bryan.**

comfort as the two depleted companies manned a defensive perimeter around the MACV compound on the South Side. The successful defense of the MACV compound on the South Side, and the concurrent defense of the 1st ARVN Division HQ compound in the northern part of Hue unhinged Communist defensive plans. Helicopters could, and did, land

platoon reinforcements at these two points. Both then served as bases from which to begin the counterattack to recapture the city. Instead of having a secure perimeter along fixed lines, the Communists had to defend against multiple threats including eruptions from within what they had thought would be their defensive perimeter. This was the significance of the gallant defense of the two strongpoints during the initial terror filled hours of the Tet Offensive. It also highlights the importance of the successful relief drive by the two Marine Corps companies during the first day.

COUNTERATTACK

One of the first Communist targets had been the jail, housing some 2,500 inmates. After liberation, about 500 of them joined the attacking forces. The attackers also captured numerous American-made weapons when they seized the ARVN armory during their opening assault. This, together with their ability to keep an open supply line from the A Shau valley, some 30 miles to the west, meant that the Communists were heavily armed and possessed ample ammunition. In addition, five reinforcing battalions joined the nine that made the initial assault. The weather too aided the Communists. Recurring misty drizzle greatly hampered Allied airpower. However, the rigid Communist plan could not adapt to the changed circumstances caused by the two Allied strongpoints within their lines. Instead of making a major effort to eliminate these positions, the attackers yielded the initiative, dug-in and awaited the Allied counterattack.

The second day in Hue, February 1, established the pattern for the remainder of the battle. The generals, from LaHue on up, spoke in

After fighting up a street, through a garden, and into a house against tough resistance, a Marine officer who had led the charge took time to inspect the enemy position. He found two-foot-thick concrete walls with bunker-style firing slits. The slits provided a perfect field of fire down the street and into the building from where the Marines had staged the assault. Stepping back, the officer could only mutter, "Son of a bitch, son of a bitch."

Flak-vested 1st Regiment Marines move a 106mm recoilless rifle into position to open the way through the next block of buildings during the house-to-house fighting in Hue.

terms of "mopping-up" and "pushing the VC out of Hue this morning." Meanwhile, three Marine companies, eventually reinforced by a fourth, began a building by building struggle through an eleven by nine block area to clear the South Side. Every alley, street corner, window, and garden wall harbored potential death. The only way to advance was to blast an entrance with bazooka or recoilless rifle fire and then send fireteams and squads into the breach. To charge through a blow-in door, clamber over an exposed garden wall, or sprint across an intersection

The Americans tended to denigrate the combat skills and bravery of their South Vietnamese allies. After-combat reports and subsequent history focused on actions featuring Americans. However, ARVN forces took the brunt of the Tet Offensive and their losses reflected this. In Saigon alone, while the American attention focused on the Embassy, racetrack and Tan Son Nhut, on the first day of battle 88 ARVN soldiers died and 239 were wounded The élite Airborne, Ranger, and Marine units suffered most of these losses. ARVN Airborne soldiers with a captured Viet Cong. In Hue the American Marines felt badly let down by the lack of contribution from the ARVN. Said one: "The ARVN were an unruly lot and they made sure to stay far to the rear of the advancing Marines ... We'd see them after a pitched battle, driving up in trucks to loot the buildings we had just captured ... I think if the ARVN ever enjoyed any fighting reputation with the Marines, they lost it in Hue."

STREET FIGHTING IN HUE

February 1–27, 1968. Typical urban combat scene as US and ARVN forces battle with NVA and VC units for control of the city.

The battle for the old Imperial Capital of Hue began on January 31 and continued until March 2, 1968. In a guerrilla war, Hue was an exception, an extended urban combat against a foe who tried to hold fixed objectives. The battle featured two NVA regiments backed by two VC sapper battalions against eight US and thirteen ARVN infantry battalions. The urban landscape denied the Allies their two greatest weapons – mobility and firepower. The battle became a savage small-unit house-to-house combat. After the first few days, the ARVN units had spent their impetus. It was left to the Marines to recapture Hue. Aided by local sympathizers and impressed civilian labor, the defenders turned each block into a fortress. They sited crew-served weapons at doorways and windows to sweep the streets; they used back alleys and lanes to hasten reinforcements to threatened sectors and to launch sudden, unexpected counterattacks. For the attackers it was a battle of fire-team rushes. Battle-scarred Patton tanks operated in the main street, but in these confined areas they were unmistakable targets for NVA machine-guns and RPGs. Holed repeatedly, the tanks would withdraw briefly. The dead and wounded crew were removed, replacement crews installed, and the tanks returned to combat. Many tanks went through several crews a day. Behind them came the flak-vested grunts. Working in close coordination with the tanks, they methodically reduced the Communist positions and clawed their way forward. From adjacent buildings, Marine scout-sniper teams tried to eliminate Communist snipers while providing covering fire for the grunts in the street. Deadly man-to-man sniper duels ensued. Jeep-mounted recoilless rifles

and Ontos antitank vehicles gave direct-fire support. Lightly armored, they utilized bold hit-and-run tactics. They would appear suddenly around a debris-clogged corner, fire, and then dash for cover. When assault up the main streets proved impossible, Marine fireteams maneuvered through back alleys to attack from the rear. Numerous garden walls and hedgerows made such tactics difficult. To work up courage for the assault, many Marine teams chanted in unison as they awaited the signal to charge. A bazooka round provided

this signal when it blasted a hole in the masonry wall separating one garden from another. Then the assault teams rushed through the breach. Too often the first through the breach fell to the defender's withering automatic weapons fire.

Both sides utilized CS tear gas rounds. Thus the battle was one of the few of the war where the presence of gas forced the combatants to fight wearing gas masks. Hue was urban combat at its worst. A day's advance was measured in yards.

NVA counterattack force guided by locals infiltrating Marines' positions

Stretcher team trying to reach wounded

Reserve fire team pinned down

106mm recoilless rifle for direct-fire support

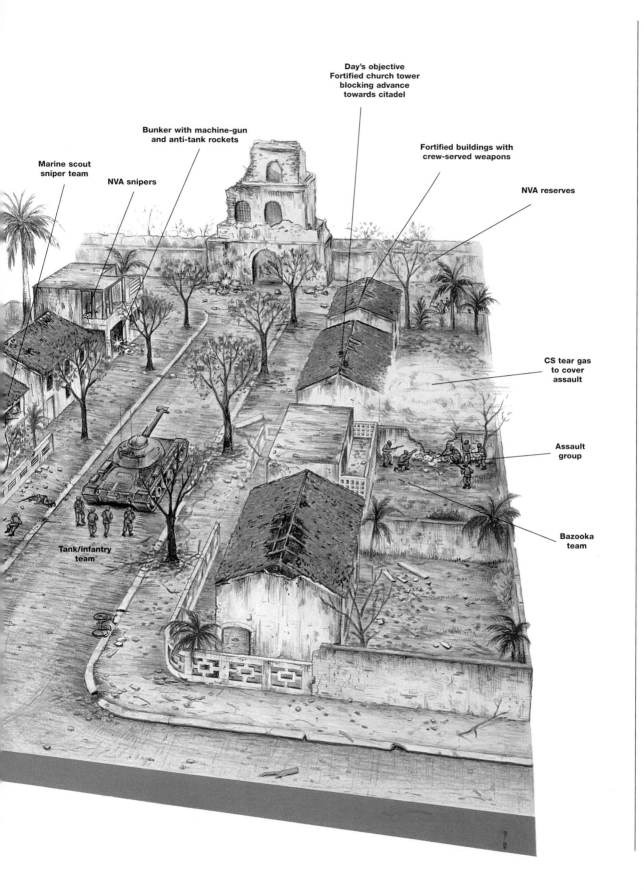

Day's objective
Fortified church tower
blocking advance
towards citadel

Bunker with machine-gun
and anti-tank rockets

Fortified buildings with
crew-served weapons

Marine scout
sniper team

NVA snipers

NVA reserves

CS tear gas
to cover
assault

Assault
group

Bazooka
team

Tank/infantry
team

required great bravery. The Marines' special *esprit de corps* motivated the 18- and 19-year-old grunts to do these things and more, repeatedly, for nearly a month.

In times past, a wounded Marine expected to receive medical evacuation and an extended recovery period. In Hue, those suffering from any but the most disabling wounds commonly were patched up by medical personnel and voluntarily returned to duty. A company leader later wrote: "I had several men who had shrapnel in legs and arms and hobbled around and begged me not to medevac them." Another officer thought that "it was payback time" for the Marines who had endured prior months of sniper fire and booby traps without being able to hit back. The presence of every rifle-wielding grunt was badly needed. Since the High Command seriously underestimated their opposition, the attackers received paltry reinforcements. For most of the long battle, a mere two understrength battalions conducted the advance. A frustrated battalion commander wondered: "Why must they always piecemeal us into battle?"

While the Marines operated on the South Side, Lieutenant General Hoang Xuam Lam worked to recapture the Citadel. He planned to use the 1st ARVN Division HQ's perimeter as a base of operations. First he needed to send reinforcements, and this proved very hard. The 7th ARVN Armored Cavalry and two airborne battalions had to force a convoy through a major ambush to reach Hue. Similarly, two battalions of the 1st ARVN Division's 3rd Regiment took fearful losses during their approach march. During February 1, the 2nd ARVN Airborne Battalions and the 7th ARVN Cavalry recaptured Tay Loc Airfield, but only after suffering heavy losses including twelve armored vehicles and the death of the cavalry squadron commander. Facing resistance every bit as tough as that confronting the American Marines across the river, the South Vietnamese slowly advanced through well-prepared fortified positions. By February 4, a battalion of the 3rd ARVN Regiment – a regiment that would consistently fight harder than any other ARVN formation and take crippling losses as a result – stormed the An Hoa gate taking the Citadel's northwest wall. This effort consumed the aggressive spirit of the airborne and regular ARVN forces. On the night of February 6, a ferocious nocturnal NVA counterattack by storm troops using grappling hooks drove the ARVN forces from the recently recaptured southwest wall.

THE FIRST TEAM

Meanwhile, outside Hue, a battalion of the hard-fighting 1st Air Cavalry Division air-assaulted into the middle of the Communist supply line in an effort to interdict the flow of supplies to Hue. Attacking through the fog, 2/12 Cav had to do without its customary helicopter gunship and aerial rocket artillery support. Confronted with two dug-in NVA battalions, the cavalry failed and retired to prepare against the expected counterattacks.

At dawn a heavy mortar barrage landed within the 150-yard-wide battalion perimeter. Charging NVA infantry, firing their AK-47s from the hip and supported by numerous machine-guns giving grazing support fire, followed the bombardment with repeated assaults. Only accurate defensive fire from a 105mm battery preserved the position.

As the afternoon wore on, casualties mounted as mortar rounds scored direct hits within the crowded perimeter. The cavalry's ammunition ran low. Medevac helicopters were able to rescue only the most seriously wounded in the face of heavy Communist fire. As nightfall approached, the battalion commander, Lieutenant Colonel Dick Sweet, realized that his isolated unit could not hold out. Sweet made a bold decision. Rather than await the final NVA assault, his unit would break out from their perimeter. Furthermore, instead of heading in the expected direction toward the nearest friendly unit, the cavalry set out across an exposed rice paddy. The most reliable point man led

A Patton tank supports the 1/5 Marines beside the citadel walls on February 12.

the way. As Private Hector Comacho recalls: "It was dark, but I trusted myself. The hardest part was finding some place where everyone could go, and making sure that everyone could keep up." Officers instructed the troopers not to fire under any circumstances, and if they received fire they were to hit the ground and remain silent. Sweet recalls the march: "We had men who had refused to be medevaced that afternoon. They hid their wounds so they could stay with the battalion … You'd see them limping; there was no talk. No noise at all. I've never seen such discipline in a unit … You'd find that the man up ahead of you who was dragging a foot had a bullet in his leg, and had it there for almost 24 hours. That's why the night march worked."

Taking all their wounded with them, the troopers trudged through a rainy, cold, pitch-black night. After a perilous eleven-hour march, 2/12 Cav arrived atop a low hill from where they could receive helicopter resupply. It had been exceedingly well done, but still the cavalry had failed to shut off the Communist flow of supplies into Hue.

HOUSE-TO-HOUSE COMBAT

Back in the city, the difficult house-to-house fighting frustrated the Allied commanders. Prohibitions on the use of artillery and air strikes, intended to preserve historic sites within Hue, coupled with poor weather limited Allied progress. On February 9, a reporter asked the commander of the 1st ARVN Division whether the Imperial Palace, which served as a defensive strongpoint, was not too important to bomb. General Truong pragmatically replied: "You exaggerate. It is good for tourists, but if we meet heavy resistance we will use air strikes, artillery, everything."

Still, the poor weather and the special Rules of Engagement employed in Hue meant that the Marines went without their customary fire support. Fortunately the big Patton tanks and the 106mm recoilless rifles provided accurate direct-fire weapons to reduce a sniper's lair or a machine-gun nest. First though, these positions had to be located, and this was usually done at cost. A Marine recalls watching a decimated platoon huddle beneath one of the ubiquitous garden walls. Several boosted one grunt over the wall. As his head reached the top a concealed AK-47 fired. The grunt flopped to the ground. He had been shot in the face. Crying out "Momma!" he died.

By February 10 the Marines had cleared the South Side. Now they had to turn their attention to the Citadel across the river. Higher command back at Phu Bai remained badly out of touch with reality. For example, its plan called for crossing a bridge that had been destroyed by NVA sappers one week earlier. Although ARVN forces had cleared about three-quarters of the Citadel, the NVA still held formidable positions and retained a functioning supply line to their strongholds in the 82 western mountains. In addition they struck back with bold counterattacks whenever possible. Indicative of their fighting spirit was a spectacular nocturnal raid by VC combat-swimmers, who mined another important river bridge and dropped two of its spans into the water.

Reinforcements arrived for the drive against the Citadel. Vietnamese Marines, having just finished clearing Saigon of VC resistance, arrived to relieve the battered airborne battalions. The US 1/5 Marines entered battle on February 12. The street fighting chewed the battalion up as witnessed by its losses among platoon leaders. After nine days of combat,

M50A1 Ontos of 3rd Anti-Tank Battalion, US Marine Corps. Illustration by Peter Sarson and Tony Bryan.

its ten rifle platoons, which would normally be led by first lieutenants, were commanded by three second lieutenants, one gunnery sergeant, two staff sergeants, two buck sergeants, and two senior corporals.

On February 26, soldiers moving through the Gia Hoi High School yard came across freshly turned earth. They investigated and uncovered the bound bodies of numerous civilians. They were the first of a colossal number of victims of a Communist atrocity, the dimensions of which were not fully appreciated until mid-1970 when the last graves were found. Around Hue, searchers eventually found 2,810 bodies, while nearly 2,000 more remained missing. Apparently the slaughter began when the VC first occupied Hue. Special commandos had rounded up and executed civilians on a blacklist of government workers and politicians. When it appeared that the Communists might be able to hold Hue, a second wave of executions took place. This time the victims were intellectuals and students who seemed to represent a threat to the new Communist order. When it became clear that the battle was going adversely, the largest number of killings occurred. The VC systematically killed anyone who might be able to identify the local Communists who had surfaced during the offensive. Following the mass killings, they tried to hide their work. Preoccupied by the ongoing combat the Allies failed to publicize the atrocity. The Press tended to disbelieve the early reports of mass graves, since these came from sources they considered discredited. Instead reporters concentrated on stories of Allied setbacks and pictures of the urban destruction.

The difficulty of the first assaults against the Citadel equaled anything in Marine Corps history. Tanks could barely manage to operate in the narrow alleys near the Citadel's high walls and towers. Wide-scale use of debilitating CS gas helped, but a day's advance frequently did not exceed 200 yards. The Marines paid in blood for most of these gains. During the week of February 13–20, four Marine companies suffered 47 killed, 240 seriously wounded, and another 60 wounded who remained in combat. Casualties were so high that the Marines sent replacements directly from their instructional camps in the United States. Hopelessly maladroit for the complex city fighting, they died far too often. Yet the relentless advance by the flak-vested grunts forced the defenders to face the inevitable. On February 16, radio intercept technicians decoded a message from the NVA commander inside Hue. It spoke of heavy losses, including the senior officer, and requested permission to withdraw. Communist HQ sent the reply to remain and fight.

By February 21 the Allies could see the end. The 1st Cavalry had managed to close the enemy supply lines into Hue. By the following day the US Marines could prepare for a final push and reported lighter enemy contact than on any previous day. Similarly, ARVN forces resumed the advance. By order of the high command, the Marines allowed the 1st ARVN Division's Black Panther Company – a unit that had fought long and hard, an exception, most Marines thought – to make the final assault. The Black Panthers charged right at the Imperial Palace, yelling and firing as they advanced, some carrying scaling ladders to get over the walls. NVA resistance had collapsed. The ARVN soldiers hauled down the Viet Cong flag that had flown for 25 days. Unaware of the ARVN contribution at Hue, a Marine officer bitterly observed: "The MACV records will reflect that the ARVN … took the Citadel. That was strictly public relations hogwash … The 1st Battalion, 5th Marines, took the Citadel. The ARVN were spectators."

Hue was the longest sustained infantry battle the war had so far seen. By Vietnam standards, losses had been high. During 26 days of combat ARVN units lost 384 killed and more than 1,800 wounded; US Army casualties were 74 dead and 507 wounded; the three Marine battalions, 142 and 857, respectively. The Allies claimed to have killed over 5,000 and captured 89. Civilian losses, both victims of Communist atrocity and hapless targets caught in the urban crossfire, amounted to some 5,800 killed. Much of the once-beautiful city of Hue lay in rubble.

Grunts belonging to "A" Company, 1/1 Marines, leave a recaptured church on February 9.

ASSESSMENT

During the preceding 25 years, the American military had made a habit of playing the victim for enemy surprise attacks. Pearl Harbor, Kasserine Pass, the Battle of the Bulge, and the Chinese intervention along the Yalu River had all caught the Americans unawares. The synchronized violence of the Tet Offensive was matched perhaps only by the Germans' Ardennes Offensive. Of all these surprise attacks, only the Tet Offensive achieved decisive results.

Yet, by conventional military calculation, Tet was an enormous Allied success. At a cost of some 4,000 Americans killed and wounded and between 4,000 and 8,000 ARVN soldiers killed, the Communists suffered 40,000 to 50,000 battlefield deaths. Most importantly, large numbers of irreplaceable local Viet Cong fighters and cadres had died. Simply put, the enemy had concentrated, and his masses had been consumed by American firepower. This battlefield success has been obscured by the more important political consequences of the Tet Offensive. However, Tet was part of an unbroken record forged by the American soldier from 1965 to 1973 of not losing a single important battle. As Douglas Pike, one of the few experts to study and comprehend the Viet Cong and North Vietnamese, notes: "Had the Vietnam War been another conventional war, had it been decided on the basis of past wars, it would have been over by mid-1968 with the defeat of the Communist forces." Indeed, the way the public perceived the battle astonished many American veterans. Standing next to enemy corpses stacked like cordwood outside his unit's headquarters, a cavalry officer wondered how: "To our complete bewilderment in the weeks that followed, nobody ever publicized this feat of battlefield triumph. Instead, we read that we had been defeated!"

It is also important to remember that the Communist strategists had designed the offensive to impress the South Vietnamese rather than the American public. A top North Vietnamese General, Tran Do, commented after the war:

"We didn't achieve our main objective, which was to spur uprisings throughout the south. Still, we inflicted heavy casualties ... As for making an impact in the United States, it had not been our intention – but it turned out to be a fortunate result."

In many ways the embassy battle was a microcosm of the entire war. The weapons and explosives used during the attack easily slipped past the hopelessly inadequate South Vietnamese security cordon around the capital. The guerrillas mustered in a building owned by a female Viet Cong agent of thirteen years' standing who had been arrested several times for subversive activities. Yet her building was not under surveillance. The attackers received help from an embassy driver, whom the Americans had often jokingly said "must be a VC" because he was so smart. They drove past South Vietnamese police who ran rather than

President Nguyen Van Thieu
places a commemorative plaque
for the victims of the Hue
massacre in 1971.

sound the alarm. In the attack the VC hardly proved supermen. They were inadequately briefed, opened fire too soon, and showed no initiative once their leaders fell.

Interestingly enough, the Communist high command had not appreciated the potential psychological impact of the embassy assault. It was just one, rather minor, target among many. In fact, the general who commanded the Saigon offensives criticized the embassy attack several days after it took place. He believed it had been poorly conceived. Only when they understood the attack's impact on the American public did the Communists begin to propagandize it. Here was the paradox of the war: a small, ill-conceived, tactically flawed attack against an insignificant military objective, designed to impress the South Vietnamese, proved the decisive action of the war because of its impact on the American public.

Communist planners had timed the offensive for a holiday period when the South Vietnamese and Americans would be less vigilant. Conveniently, it was also at a critical time in the United States. It was just before the first presidential primaries and thus, in the words of Don Oberdorfer, "caught the American political system at its moment of greatest irresolution and potential for change." Incomplete, inaccurate, and biased Press coverage of the combat influenced the public's perception. However, even if this type of coverage were discounted, the public recognized by the widespread and ferocious nature of the Tet Offensive that the enemy remained much stronger than their politicians and generals had led them to believe. The choice seemed to be to escalate yet again or to seek terms.

The first option seemed unpromising because strategically the Tet Offensive undercut Westmoreland's attrition strategy. The essential weakness of this strategy should have been apparent before Tet. In mid-1967 the NVA comprised some 450,000 men of whom a mere 70,000 served in Laos and South Vietnam. Each year about 200,000 young men reached the age of eighteen. Simple arithmetic could show that the Communists had the manpower to endure the kind of terrible losses they suffered in 1967 for years to come. If attrition strategy could not kill the enemy fast enough, in spite of amazing favorable kill ratios of 10 to 1 or better, then the outcome hinged on will. Recent history against the French, let alone the long history of Vietnamese resistance to the Chinese, clearly demonstrated that Communist morale, which had assumed the mantle of stubborn Vietnamese nationalism, would not crack.

If escalation would not work, negotiation seemed the only alternative. Many historians point to the night of February 27, 1968 as a turning point in the war. That evening, the popular and much-respected American broadcaster Walter Cronkite delivered a televised special report summing up the Tet Offensive. Cronkite had just returned from a whirlwind tour of South Vietnam and what he had seen had greatly depressed him. He began his report in the most despairing manner. While the camera panned over battle damage in Saigon, he intoned that the ruins "in this burned and blasted and weary land … mean success or setback, victory or defeat, depending on who you talk to." He proceeded to juxtapose official comments minimizing setbacks with selected eyewitness accounts that claimed disaster. He left no doubt what he personally felt, using such terms as "the shattered pieces" of pacification, stating that the South Vietnamese government "could salvage a measure of victory from defeat." His interviews and film seemed to discredit all official pronouncements. Cronkite concluded:

"We have been too often disappointed by the optimism of the American leaders … To say that we are closer to victory today is to

The "Mini Tet" Offensive in May brought a return to street fighting in Saigon.

believe, in the face of the evidence, the optimists who have been wrong in the past … To say that we are mired in stalemate seems the only realistic, yet unsatisfactory, conclusion … it is increasingly clear to this reporter that the only rational way out will be to negotiate, not as victors, but as an honorable people who lived up to their pledge to defend democracy, and did the best they could."

Initially, Press reports including Cronkite's did little to alter the public's attitude toward the war. Whereas before Tet 45 percent believed that sending American troops to Vietnam was a mistake, 49 percent felt this way after Tet. More important, the extremely influential Eastern television and print media moguls, and substantial numbers of the Washington, DC, opinion makers and politicians, concluded that the war was lost. They began to disseminate this message to the country, and the public listened. Consequently, February and March led to a turning point in American opinion about the war. During the two months following Tet, one in every five Americans switched from pro- to anti-war. Johnson's popularity among both pro- and anti-war people plummeted. Public frustration encompassed roughly equal numbers of hawks – who were angered at the administration's half-measures that seemed only to produce more dead American boys – and the doves who simply wanted to get out.

The American Press played a decisive role in the Tet Offensive. Yet, in both detail, analysis and conclusion, Press reporting of the Tet

Offensive was highly misleading. An inexperienced, or lazy, reporter covering the war from the comfort of Saigon could not understand how the Communists had been able to mass for their surprise assaults without detection. They reported that it must be because of a sympathetic civilian population who helped conceal Communist movements. Here was more evidence, ran a common Press refrain, to undermine the administration's claims about the war's progress.

In fact, the majority of the South Vietnamese civilian population was neutral, more interested in survival than anything else. The Communists needed little assistance beyond that provided by their local cadres, who represented a small percentage of the total population. The terrain provided the rest. Even Saigon lay surrounded by swamps, woods, and canals. The Communists took advantage of this concealment to march in secret to staging areas on the city's outskirts. But this important fact was unknown to the majority of the Press and so remained unreported to the public. The public could only conclude that an obliging citizenry had escorted the enemy to the gates of the American bases. Similarly, the Press had few contacts within the South Vietnamese military. The handful of reports that did focus on ARVN performance highlighted those units and leaders who had fought the poorest. This message reinforced the growing sense that America fought alone.

At the time, political and military leaders from Johnson and Westmoreland down blamed the Press for losing the war. The effort continued for years thereafter as discredited leaders sought to recover prestige. But their carping obscures the fact already described that even with a fully muzzled Press America had no viable war-winning strategy.

By the end of March the domestic sea change led to the announcement by the proud, embittered President Lyndon Johnson that he would not run for re-election. In an effort at negotiated settlement, Americans and North Vietnamese met in Paris in mid-May 1968, some three months after Tet. American leaders never fully comprehended the masterful Communist negotiating strategy of "fighting and talking." More Americans would be killed after the "peace talks" opened than before they began.

On July 3, General William Westmoreland departed as MACV commander to become the new Army Chief of Staff. Few doubted that, defeated and discredited, he had been kicked upstairs. Responding to domestic political pressure, his replacement – General Creighton Abrams – ordered sweeping strategic changes. American tactical aggressiveness gave way to the new mandate to reduce American battlefield casualties. Equally important, the high command decided that, henceforth, South Vietnamese troops would switch from pacification to mainstream combat. This decision, formally announced by the Joint Chiefs of Staff on April 16, 1968, marked the beginning of what would become the ill-fated "Vietnamization" policy. Thus the Tet Offensive achieved a certain symmetry of results: it destroyed the Viet Cong but caused the Americans to begin to disengage as they turned the war over to the South Vietnamese. The future would depend on the contest between the regulars of North and South Vietnam.

Meanwhile, in selected areas American soldiers would continue offensive operations. But the nature of the war changed. Abrams, much to the disgust of more junior, hard-charging officers, responded to new political realities by emphasizing city security. He badly wanted to avoid a repeat of the Saigon and Hue battles. The need to defend cities took manpower away from offensive action. None the less, adequate ARVN-US planning for Saigon's defense did not take place until after the second major Communist assault exploded through the capital in May.

The Tet Offensive demonstrated to many the essential dilemma the American military faced in Vietnam: "Guerrillas win if they don't lose. A standard army loses if it does not win." Even this comment obscures the most important facet of the war: first and foremost it was a political struggle. The Communists clearly recognized this from the beginning and wove an integrated military/political war-winning strategy. American politicians refused to mobilize the political will of the country, meddled with military strategy to its profound detriment but, in the end, listened to the generals who claimed they could conquer on the battlefield. The military, in turn, did not appreciate the political consequences of what it did. They had some understanding of domestic American consequences, but little regard for the impact of operations on the citizens of Vietnam. A North Vietnamese officer, explaining why America lost, put it most plainly: "Your second weak point was to try to win the hearts and minds of the people while you were using bombs to kill them."

During the Tet Offensive the American military had achieved notable successes and suffered some important failures. In spite of advance warning, Westmoreland had failed to alert adequately all units before the enemy assault. He was caught in mid-shift of major formations northward. He underestimated the psychological importance of Saigon and Hue. He failed to establish a coordinated ARVN-US plan for city defense.

Scenes of urban death and destruction once again provided film for television cameras. Vietnamese Rangers collect the bodies of slain Viet Cong in June 1968.

Tactically, the surprise offensive caught the Allies short of weapons and lacking appropriate tactics for urban warfare. The military had consciously discarded many of the heavier weapons associated with conventional combat in order to improve mobility in Vietnam's hinterland. Suddenly forced into tough house-to-house fighting, soldiers found themselves without direct-fire heavy weapons such as the Marine's 106mm recoilless rifle. They had to rely upon helicopter gunships, air strikes and artillery, all of which were less accurate and increased destruction of civilian life and property.

Tet was a major setback for the slowly improving South Vietnamese military. Along with their advisers, ARVN units fought unaided on the ground in 36 of 44 provincial capitals, 64 of 242 district capitals, and 50 hamlets attacked at the beginning of Tet. The best units acquitted themselves very well during the fighting. Some poorly regarded divisions fought much better then expected. Others, such as the 2nd Division at Quang Ngai which had been judged combat effective, displayed little fighting spirit. Overall, the units that fought the best suffered serious losses and declined as a result of Tet. The official casualty count probably understated South Vietnamese losses: 4,954 killed, 15,097 wounded, 926 missing. Unofficial estimates counted at least double this total of soldiers killed.

The stunning violence of the Communist assault demonstrated to South Vietnamese civilians that their own government, supported by the Americans and despite their weapons and promises, could not protect them. The Communist occupation of the old Imperial City of Hue had an adverse impact on South Vietnamese morale comparable to the American public's reaction to the embassy attack. Nationwide war-weariness set in and desertion rates soared. At the end of 1967 the desertion rate was 10.5 per thousand. After heavy fighting and new mobilization orders, the July 1968 rate was 16.5 per thousand. Some 13,506 men deserted in July alone.

The Tet Offensive was also a bad setback for the pacification effort. More than one-third of the ARVN regular battalions assigned to pacification in rural areas had to withdraw into nearby cities. In the absence of protection, half the rural development teams, who had been making some progress at winning popular support for the government, abandoned their villages. These teams were the lynchpin of the pacification effort, which, in turn, was fundamental to Allied strategy.

From the Communist perspective, on the battlefield Tet had achieved far less than had been hoped. The Hanoi command had seemingly overestimated the readiness of the southern people to rise and overthrow the government. Giap had apparently yielded to impatience and misjudged the situation. The months following the offensive witnessed a doctrinal debate within the Hanoi Command. A key conclusion was that victory could be achieved by remaining in Mao's Stage Two of guerrilla war without ever massing for Stage Three combat. This conclusion was a dramatic departure from previous doctrine.

The war would now be won by the "super-guerrilla." This fighter was anything but the black-pyjama-clad, lightly armed, local guerrilla. Rather he was a well-trained fighting man armed with the best weapons that the Communist world could provide. He used modern communications equipment to coordinate his effort, and would conduct deadly raids against enemy installations in order to limit the enemy's initiative and wear him down. Doctrine aside, however, such were the Tet losses that the Communists were unable to launch any major attacks during 1969.

The Tet Offensive, along with the subsequent summer offensives, nearly annihilated the Viet Cong. The VC suffered irreplaceable losses among key leaders and agents. As one survivor lamented: "We lost our best people." Henceforth, the North Vietnamese would have to bear the brunt of all combat operations. Combined VC/ NVA casualties had been so severe that they required four years to recover before launching another major offensive. Even then, the Easter offensive of 1972 relied upon NVA soldiers for 90 percent of the combat.

Given the important differences between Hanoi's and the National Liberation Front's objectives, the destruction of the Viet Cong was not entirely unwelcome in the North. The Offensive killed off many leaders who might have challenged Northern hegemony. Events after the war support this dark view of Hanoi's strategy. Many surviving high-ranking Viet Cong were terribly disheartened at what befell their movement. They felt betrayed by their northern brothers. Some had to flee the county. Northern historians, on the other hand, minimized the importance of the VC's contribution. Some virtually denied that the NLF and the VC had much to do with the war. While as of 1989, Hanoi has apparently solid control over the country, according to reports from people who flee the country, strife between north and south still simmers beneath the surface. From the Viet Cong perspective, Tet must be seen as a terrible bloodbath, a catastrophic defeat.

For the North Vietnamese, Tet marked the turn of the tide. But this was not readily appreciated at the time. Responding to a question of whether the High Command knew they had won the war in 1968, a general replied: "Yes and no. Nixon began the withdrawal, but Vietnamization was a difficult period for us ... 1969 and 1970 were very hard on us. The fighting was very fierce."

While Communist post-mortems of many of the attacks, particularly those in Saigon, were full of honest self-criticism, Hue was deemed a battle whose "most outstanding feature was that we won an overall success." The Communist command was particularly pleased to note that "Hue was the place where reactionary spirit had existed for over ten years. However, it took us only a short time to drain it to its root." Without apologies, such was the Viet Cong view of civilian massacre.

Whether the Communists could have endured an Allied counter-offensive during 1968 of the type proposed by Westmoreland is one of the tantalizing "what ifs" of the Vietnam War. But as memories of the war's horror fade with time, and generals propound theories on how it could have been won, recall the words of a North Vietnamese officer who acknowledged the terrible losses suffered during Tet: "We had hundreds of thousands killed in this war. We would have sacrificed one or two million more if necessary."

The Tet Offensive of 1968 failed to defeat the American combat soldier on the battlefield, but it had defeated his general's strategy, his political leaders, and reversed the support of the people back home. It was one of the few battles of history that can be called decisive.

PART 2

KHE SANH
1967 - 68

VIETNAM STRATEGIC SITUATION, 1968

C H I N A

NORTH VIETNAM

Red River

Dien Bien Phu

● Hanoi

GULF OF TONKIN

HAINAN I.

Mekong

L
A
O
S

Vientiane

DMZ

Khe Sanh
Hue ●

CTZ I

SOUTH
CHINA
SEA

THAILAND

C A M B O D I A

CTZ II

Phnom Penh ●

CTZ III

SOUTH VIETNAM

● Saigon

GULF

OF

SIAM

Mekong

CTZ IV

Mekong Delta

N

– – – CTZ	Corps Tactical Zone
—— DMZ	Demiliartized Zone

0   100 miles

0   200 km

ORIGINS OF THE CAMPAIGN

The campaign on the Khe Sanh plateau spanned a period of over a year and was essentially a series of interconnected battles. None of the battles was strategically decisive, but they attracted a great deal of attention as the media focused on this small, remote plateau and drew endless comparisons with the French defeat at Dien Bien Phu 12 years earlier. The press repeatedly predicted the defeat of the Marines throughout the 77-day siege of Khe Sanh Combat Base (KSCB), but the Marines took a somewhat different view – to them it was "the so-called siege."

Khe Sanh was a small village in the extreme northwest of the Republic of Vietnam (South Vietnam). It was located in Quang Tri, the northernmost province of South Vietnam whose northern border ran along the Demilitarized Zone (DMZ) separating South Vietnam from the Democratic Republic of Vietnam (North Vietnam). This area was remote, sparsely populated, and a focal point of the war effort in 1968. North Vietnamese Army (NVA) forces were infiltrating the south in ever greater numbers, escalating the war and raising the stakes.

A string of US Marine Corps and Vietnamese combat bases had been established south of the DMZ to protect the population centers and the lines of communication along the coast. The Marine forces were part of III Marine Amphibious Force (III MAF), which was responsible for over 81,000 troops in January 1968. Also in the northern portion of South Vietnam was the Army of the Republic of Vietnam's (ARVN) I Corps Tactical Zone (I CTZ). Most of the ARVN forces were concentrated on the populous coastal plain, with some deployed in the hills that stretched inland. Only a small base at Khe Sanh secured the westernmost sector, some 30 kilometers (19 miles) of rugged country stretching from the Marine combat bases at the "Rockpile" and Ca Lu to the Laotian border. Khe Sanh had only one line of communication, National Route 9 (QL9 – *Quoc Lo 9*) running east–west between Quang Tri Province and Laos. This "National Route" consisted in reality of a one-lane dirt road that crossed scores of streams along its route and as a result was all too easily cut by the enemy. The hills and forests that characterized northwest Quang Tri Province concealed enemy movements and the many bridges were vulnerable in the extreme and easy to destroy, with few alternative routes available through the deep gorges. To exacerbate the situation, the weather conditions predominantly favored the enemy.

The North Vietnamese were taking advantage of the porous nature of the US/ARVN defenses in this remote area to infiltrate large numbers of troops and supplies into South Vietnam through Laos via the Ho Chi Minh Trail. The "Trail" was actually a network of roads and pathways running from North Vietnam south through Laos and Cambodia into the Republic of Vietnam. The heavily wooded and hilly terrain, sparse population, weak Free World forces, and natural infiltration routes put the NVA in a very strong position in this region.

The battle for Khe Sanh is often depicted as purely a Marine Corps operation, but the reality was very different. US Army forces, including the 1st Cavalry Division (Airmobile), were assigned to the defense of the KSCB alongside Marine units and were also heavily committed to relief and support operations in the area. US Army Special Forces and ARVN units were also involved and US Air Force, Marine Corps, US Navy and Vietnamese Air Force aircraft were heavily committed in the close air support, bombing, reconnaissance, resupply, and medical evacuation (medevac) roles.

What about Dien Bien Phu?

Throughout the Khe Sanh campaign the media maintained insistent and dogmatic comparisons of Khe Sanh with the disastrous French defeat at Dien Bien Phu in 1954, with almost constant predictions that the Marine base would fall at any moment. Almost 40 percent of the stories filed in February and March 1968 dealt with Khe Sanh. While there are undoubted similarities between the two battles, a rational assessment, even without the advantages of hindsight, should have demonstrated that both tactically and strategically the two situations bore little comparison. It is clear that, as with the French at Dien Bien Phu, the US held a fortified position centered on an airfield in a remote valley, surrounded by mountainous terrain deep inside hostile territory. The Free World troops, like the French, were cut off from overland communications and relied solely on aerial resupply, making heavy demands of available air assets. Effective close air support was critical in both instances, with the enemy deployed on hills overlooking the strongholds and freely able to fire artillery into them – artillery duels were almost constant in both cases. On both occasions the defending forces lost exposed outlying positions: Strongpoint "Gabrielle" in the case of Dien Bien Phu, and Khe Sanh village and Lang Vei Special Forces Camp outside Khe Sanh Combat Base. The weather also played a major part in both operations. While the similarities were real and too obvious for the media to resist drawing comparisons, at the level of military operations, they were largely superficial.

The French base at Dien Bien Phu had been much more remote from its supporting base, some 200 kilometers distant. Khe Sanh was only 45km from its support base, barely a 20-minute helicopter flight. At Dien Bien Phu the French position had been dominated by enemy-controlled hills completely surrounding the base, with much of the Viet Minh artillery within 3–5km. At Khe Sanh the Marines occupied the key hills dominating the base to a distance of as much as 7km, forcing the NVA to deploy their artillery between 9 and 13km away, although mortars were able to move in

Khe Sanh Combat Base viewed from the east looking the length of the runway. The outer perimeter at the photograph's bottom is the 37th ARVN Ranger Battalion's line. Behind it and curving back to the left is the Marines' Gray Sector. The Blue Sector parallels the right edge. The dark area off the right end of the road running toward the bottom of the photograph from the parking area and adjacent to the runway is ASP No. 1 (ammo dump). The FOB-3 compound is in the upper left.

Many feared that Khe Sanh would be a repeat of Dien Bien Phu. Here victorious Viet Minh raise their flag over the French former command post in Strongpoint Claudine, May 8, 1954.

closer. Despite possessing artillery that was lighter and of shorter range than that at Khe Sanh, the Viet Minh had more than 200 pieces of artillery, including mortars, at Dien Bien Phu; this was many more than the NVA had at its disposal around Khe Sanh. The Marines at the Combat Base had some 30 tubes at their disposal and were additionally supported by four batteries of 175mm guns further east. The French at Dien Bien Phu had no external artillery support, and of their 48 artillery pieces half were short-ranged heavy mortars, and some were lost in the first days. With the exception of the four hill positions to the north, Khe Sanh was concentrated in a 400–600 by 2,300 meter area, while the French positions at Dien Bien Phu sprawled across a 2,600 by 3,000 meter area with three large outlying strongpoints. Khe Sanh's smaller size allowed it to be defended by a much smaller force. Dien Bien Phu was densely packed with troops and proved difficult to defend. Just 6,680 troops defended Khe Sanh, six battalions counting Forward Operations Base 3 (FOB-3) and the tiny Ranger battalion, of which three were defending the hill outposts. Dien Bien Phu held 16,500 troops, 19 infantry battalions (including later parachute-delivered reinforcements), making supply extremely difficult.

The French needed 150 tons of aerial resupply per day requiring 80 transport aircraft sorties. On average they delivered 117–123 tons, of which 100 were usable. They had only 75 combat aircraft and 100 transports and reconnaissance aircraft available, and the French C-47s had a payload of only 4 tons, while US C-130Es and C-123Ks carried 13 and 5 tons respectively. When the French fought at Dien Bien Phu there were 54 helicopters in all of French Indochina; the US had over 3,300 in 1967–68. A total of 9,109 Marine helicopter sorties transported 14,562 passengers and 4,661 tons of cargo to Khe Sanh, while Air Force transports delivered over 14,000 tons of cargo. The French conducted around 10,400 aircraft sorties of all types to support the 167-day siege; the US sometimes exceeded 2,500 sorties a day across South Vietnam. The French required 34,000 tons of engineering materials to completely fortify Dien Bien Phu, but the garrison received only 4,000 tons. The French were hard-pressed to maintain three days' ammunition and rations, but while there were occasional shortages at Khe Sanh, a 30-day supply was maintained. The US dropped almost as much tonnage of bombs (114,810 tons) at Khe Sanh in three months as B-29s rained on Japan during 1945. Helicopter support was essential as this was the only way the hill outposts could be supplied, replacements delivered, and casualties evacuated. French aircraft losses included 48 shot down, 14 destroyed on the ground, and 167 damaged. The US losses amounted to four transports shot down and 23 Marine fixed-wing aircraft and 123 helicopters damaged, mostly superficially. Fewer than three dozen helicopters were lost and very few attack aircraft were damaged. It proved impossible to evacuate most of the wounded from Dien Bien Phu. The US evacuated 2,000 seriously wounded from Khe Sanh and fewer than 300 lightly wounded were returned to duty.

The media's "Dien Bien Phu Syndrome" regarding Khe Sanh often dwelled on the NVA tying down 6,680 Marines. Granted, Khe Sanh required extensive air support, but this did not markedly degrade the air support necessary to defeat the Tet Offensive occurring at the same time. The media's standpoint also failed to acknowledge that four, and later five, NVA divisions were being tied down by 6,680 Marines, troops that could have been used elsewhere to support the Tet Offensive. The NVA siege required massive logistical resources and sucked in a great deal of manpower, including transport and rear-area service troops. The amount of ammunition they expended on Khe Sanh could have been used against the many Free World combat bases along the DMZ and against populated areas.

Another factor that must be considered is that the defenders of Dien Bien Phu knew within three weeks of the beginning of the siege that they were in dire straits. The defenders of Khe Sanh, the grunt Marines,

Major Weapons: Khe Sanh and Dien Bien Phu

US/French	Khe Sanh	Dien Bien Phu[1]
heavy mortars	7 x 4.2in	28 x 120mm
105mm howitzers	18	24
155mm howitzers	6	4
recoilless rifles	93 x 106mm	8–12 x 75mm
tanks	6 x 90mm	10 x 76mm
quad .50-cal MGs	2	4
twin 40mm guns	2	–
Artillery expenditure (rounds)		
US/French	158,900	93,000
NVA/Viet Minh	11,114[2]	103,000[3]

Cloud-shrouded hills provide the backdrop to KSCB. This is the north perimeter trench showing fighting bunkers along the trench line. The gray-green woven plastic and tan burlap sandbag parapets against the dark red soil highlight the trench outlines. The airfield is beyond the buildings and tents in the background.

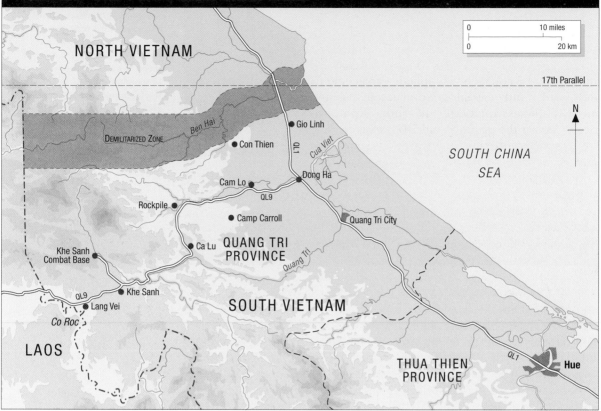

QUANG TRI PROVINCE AND DMZ

never had a doubt they would hold and were chomping at the bit to get at the enemy with offensive operations.

The French lost at least 4,000 dead or missing with over 10,000 surrendering, many of whom were wounded (figures are not always consistent or reliable because losses in the final days were not recorded). US losses at Khe Sanh were a fraction of this and are discussed in the *Aftermath* chapter of this book. Of the 49,500 Viet Minh troops at Dien Bien Phu, an estimated 7,900 were killed and 15,000 wounded.

Terrain and weather

Quang Tri ("Great Administration") was South Vietnam's most northerly province and bordered North Vietnam, its border defined by the Song (river) Ben Hai – ostensibly a demilitarized zone. With Laos lying just to the west, the area was known as the tri-border region. Stretching inland from the South China Sea coast is an approximately 30km-wide coastal plain where most of the province's population resided and where most US and ARVN forces were deployed. Running south out of Laos is the rugged Annamite Cordillera (mountain range) which cuts through the western portion of the province, stretching some 40–50km from the Laotian border. Two narrow rivers flow east out of the Annamites, the Song Cam Lo in the north running roughly parallel with and south of the DMZ, and the Song Quang Tri further south, a tributary of which, Song Rao Quan, flows past Khe Sanh. They meet on the coastal plain just east of Dong Ha, merging into the Song Cua Viet.

The Annamites rise over 5,000ft north of Khe Sanh and 2,200ft to the west. Nestled in the mountains some 60km inland is the Khe Sanh plateau, a small triangular plateau measuring around 5–6km each side. The Laotian border is some 18km to the west and the DMZ around 30km to the north. While the distances are not great, the plateau lies in an extremely remote position, accessed along a single neglected road, National Route 9 (QL9), winding through the hills and crossing dozens of streams and rivers. The road distance between Khe Sanh and Dong Ha was 63km and was dotted with 36 bridges, many bypassed because of their dilapidated condition. From Ca Lu, 18km east-northeast of Khe Sanh, QL9 was a dirt road all the way to Laos and easily cut by enemy forces concealed in the dense terrain. At a point 2km southwest of Khe Sanh, QL9 turned into a single-lane track running southwest into Laos through Khe Sanh village. A dirt road branched off at this point to run northwest to KSCB.

The major Marine base in Quang Tri was at Dong Ha, 45km to the east-northeast where QL9 connected to the north–south QL1 running south to Quang Tri City. The Marine combat bases closest to KSCB were the "Rockpile" 20km northeast and Camp "J.J. Carroll" 25km east-northeast. Over a dozen other Marine and ARVN combat bases were scattered between Carroll and the coast, protecting the coastal plain from NVA thrusts across the DMZ. QL9, running east from Laos, and the valley of the Khe Ta Hong stream, running from the northwest from the junction of the DMZ/Laotian border, both converged on the Khe Sanh plateau and were accessible from the Ho Chi Minh Trail network in Laos. Just inside Laos and parallel with Khe Sanh along QL9 was Co Roc Mountain 13km to the southwest. This large 850m ridge served as an NVA artillery position.

The Khe Sanh plateau is about 1,500ft above sea level and is generally flat, though there are low, gently rolling hills on the southern and western sides. Its northeast side is defined by the approximately 300m-deep Rao Qung gorge a few hundred meters north and east of the Khe Sanh airfield, with the narrow river itself flowing northwest to southeast. The

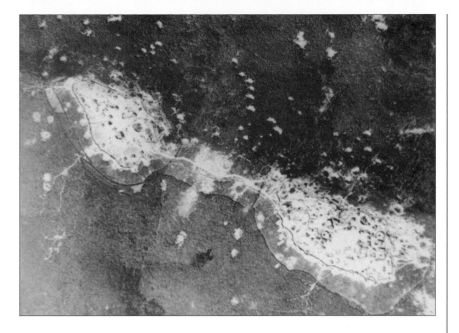

A vertical view of 881S. North is to the upper right corner. Much of the barrier wire pattern can be discerned as well as the helicopter LZ between the two peaks. Bomb craters from earlier fighting are apparent.

plateau is covered by scattered trees, brush, bamboo, 3–10ft-high elephant grass, and cultivated plots of coffee plants. On the plateau's higher elevations double-canopy rainforest dominates, with trees up to 90ft high and the second-canopy trees growing up to 60ft. Thin underbrush makes movement easy while providing cover from aerial observation. In some lower areas the ground had once been cleared, but the jungle reclaimed it; 20–40ft trees, bamboo, and underbrush cover this area, restricting movement. The hills are moderately sloped and dome-shaped, their sides cut by finger-like ridges and gorges making cross-country movement difficult. Local tracks wind throughout the area, but the dense vegetation and broken ground provide cover and concealment from air and ground observation and fire.

A ragged line of hills stretching west to east north of Khe Sanh was critical to both sides. Hill 881[4] South (881S) was 7km west-northwest of KSCB. Hill 881 North (881N), a key NVA position, lay 2km north of 881S. Hills 861 and 861A were 4km to the northwest, with the two peaks separated by a 400m saddle. Hill 558 lay 4km north-northwest of KSCB, and about 1.5km east-northeast of 861A, while Hill 950 was 4.5km due north of KSCB. Just over a kilometer to the east is Hill 1015 (Dong Tri, "Tiger Tooth Mountain"), the highest peak in the immediate area. Caves pockmarked some of the limestone hills while the soil was a rich deep volcanic red.

Some 3.5km south of KSCB was Khe Sanh village, which was the location of the Huong Hoa District (equivalent to a US county) Headquarters prior to the siege. Lang Vei Special Forces Camp was 9km southwest of KSCB, in an exposed position astride QL9. In September 1967 the camp was re-opened 1km further west, just over 2km from the Laotian border. Over 10,000 Vietnamese lived in the district in four villages with 12,000 Montagnards[5] in a half-dozen villages.

It is often argued that in warfare the weather is neutral, but it can, nevertheless, severely hamper operations dependent on good weather. Equally, poor weather conditions can be a powerful ally to a force operating with limited resources and relying on undetected movement. At Khe Sanh the Marines depended heavily on favorable weather to enable them to observe and detect enemy troops and artillery, which in turn allowed these to be targeted by US ground-attack missions. The availability of air support was essential to allow air strikes, aerial surveillance, and the delivery of supplies on which the base was totally dependent.

The siege of Khe Sanh took place between mid January and the beginning of April 1968, within the period of the northeast monsoon. For most of Southeast Asia, November to March brought dry winds from China, a period of little rain and clear skies. The northern area of South Vietnam was an exception to this general rule, as the dry winds from China collected moisture as they passed over the South China Sea. This in turn resulted in rain as the winds crossed the highlands of South Vietnam. Rather than the dry season experienced in the rest of the region, this part of Vietnam essentially had a year-round wet season. The weather on the Khe Sanh plateau and surrounding area was characterized by low clouds, fog, overcast skies, and sporadic light rains. Annual rainfall was 80in, most of it falling during the northeast monsoon.

The heavy rain was accompanied by a weather phenomenon known as the *crachin*, in which dense 3,000–5,000ft-thick cloud formations reach as low as 500ft, reducing visibility to less than half a mile. Lasting from three to five days with light rain, these periods all but precluded close air support and aerial resupply. The cloud and fog at Khe Sanh was heavier than usual during the siege. Cloud cover extended to below 2,000ft on more than half the mornings, with visibility less than 2 miles. By early afternoon the cloud would normally lift to around 3,000ft.

What the US had not appreciated was that the base itself affected the weather. Fog formed at night as the ground cooled, with the high-humidity air condensing and clouds settling on the hills and plateau. Warmer air in the Rao Qung gorge rose as the higher ground cooled and added to the fog as it condensed. At sunrise, rather than the fog burning off as was typical, the airfield's aluminum matting and surrounding bare ground warmed rapidly, drawing the now night-cooled air up from lower ground to condense and create dense morning fog over the base. The fog sometimes lifted or burned off in the late morning or early afternoon, but by late afternoon or early evening would begin forming once more as the runway cooled, again leading the moist monsoon air to condense. KSCB was itself a "fog factory." Seldom was there any more than six hours of clear sky, and even then visibility was less than 5 miles. Although not actually cold, the base could be damp and chilly, with drizzle sometimes lasting for days. Afternoons were, by contrast, often hot and humid.

Khe Sanh Combat Base

ARVN engineers had built a dirt airstrip north of Khe Sanh village in September 1962, making it the most northwestern airfield in South Vietnam (designated VA1-44). A radio relay site (Lemon Tree) had been established on Hill 950 in late 1964, protected by a rifle platoon – the first Marine combat unit deployed to Vietnam. In September 1966, Navy Mobile Construction Battalion 10 Seabees improved the 1,500ft runway, extending it to 3,300ft and adding steel planking to allow cargo aircraft

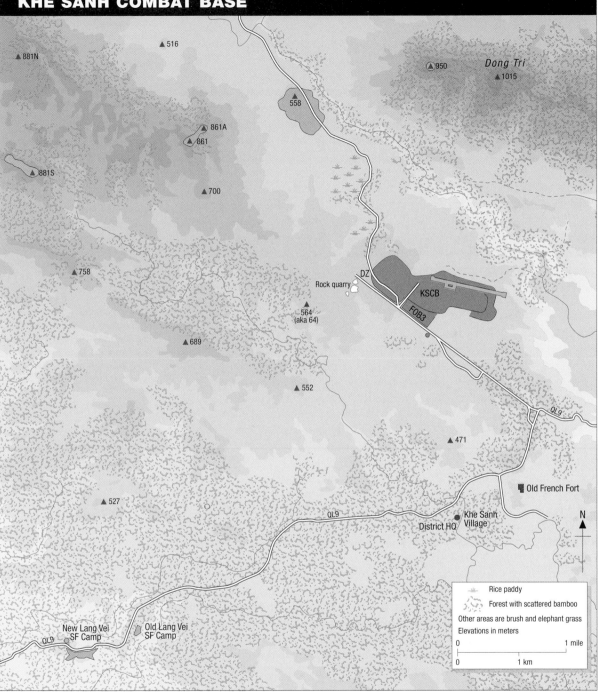

to use it. A Marine battalion occupied the airfield in October 1966, and in December 1966 the Special Forces camp (established there in July 1962 on the south central part of the strip) was relocated to Lang Vei, 9km to the southwest. Six different A-teams[6] occupied the camp on six-month rotating tours until A-101 became the permanent resident team in December 1966. From February 1967, only a single Marine company (E/2/9) garrisoned the Khe Sanh airfield until the April–May

Hill 861A, the lower near portion, and 861 were defended by E/2/26 and K/3/26 with two platoons A/1/26, respectively. The clear light spot between the two main positions is a helicopter LZ. The NVA attacks of January 21 and February 6 came up the wooded slope to the right.

A thousand troops of 2/26 Marines (-) were dug-in around Hill 558 blocking the Rao Qung gorge (upper right) and a dirt road (cutting diagonally through the perimeter) approaching KSCB from the northwest. The actual Hill 558 is in the upper left. The irregular light areas are cleared swatches around the perimeter.

1967 Hill Battles. At that time KSCB bore only a passing resemblance to the fortified complex it became during the siege.

As action increased in the area, the Seabees of Naval Mobile Construction Battalion Unit 301 improved the airfield, on which the matting had buckled during the monsoon rains. They established a rock quarry one mile to the southwest, and closed the airfield on August 17, 1967. They pulled up the pierced steel planking, extended the runway to 3,895ft, laid an asphalt-bonded, crushed-rock foundation, installed 3,000 new panels of AM2 matting, and re-opened the airfield on October 27. Resupply during this period was carried out by airdrop, helicopter, and C-7A Caribous landing on short runway sections.

KSCB presented a worn, battered, cluttered appearance. Constant shelling, ongoing construction projects and repairs, haphazardly stacked materials and supplies, damaged vehicles, aircraft wreckage, piles of expended artillery cartridges, ammunition boxes, and tubes and packaging littered the base. Anything that could be used for construction materials – wooden ammunition boxes, pallets, fuel drums – were quickly put to use. Hundreds of radio antennae were scattered across the base, many of them dummies even erected over latrines in an attempt to provide a multitude of potential targets to frustrate the enemy. Miles of field telephone wire snaked through the trenches of the base.

When the base was first established a single coil of concertina wire protected the perimeter, and brush and elephant grass left poor fields of observation and fire. The barrier was upgraded and by the time of the siege it presented a formidable obstacle. Beyond hand-grenade range of the trench line was a double row of concertina razor wire[7] with a third stacked on top making the barrier 6ft high. Beyond this *fougasse* flame weapons[8] were buried at intervals, along with command-detonated M18A1 Claymore antipersonnel mines. Next was a double-apron barrier, a multi-strand barbed-wire fence with anchor wires in a "V" pattern on both sides. Across the anchor wires were placed horizontal strands creating sloping barriers – the aprons. In some sectors another double- or single-apron fence might be erected even further out. Between the barriers was strung "tanglefoot" – barbed wire set horizontally in crisscross patterns 1ft above the ground, designed to slow attackers. There were wide, clear strips between the barriers and tanglefoot. These areas were often planted with M16A1 ("bouncing betty") and M14 ("toe-popper" or "shoe polish can") antipersonnel mines as well as some M15 and M19 antitank mines. Apparently abandoned, partly used barbed-wire spools and barbed-wire pickets were left among the barriers for NVA sappers to recover. These were booby-trapped with grenades. Tripwire-activated flares were also emplaced in the barriers. These burned for about a minute, illuminating an area of 300 square meters. There were protected zigzag routes through the barriers, allowing patrols to pass through. Recovering supply pallets that had missed their target or enemy dead from within the barriers was a dangerous assignment. The barriers were difficult to maintain, with breaches caused by artillery and mortars having to be repaired, additional barriers added in some sectors, and grass burned off. The protective barriers around the various hilltop positions were not as extensive as those at KSCB; they would often consist of just one or two belts of single or double concertina wire, and it was almost impossible to clear all the vegetation. Mines and booby traps gave additional protection to these positions.

Trenches within the base varied, but were 4–6ft deep, 1–2ft wide at the bottom, and 2–3ft wide at the top. The soil was sufficiently stable that few of the trench sections required strengthening with sandbags. The spoil from the trench was heaped to either side and the parapet raised with between one and three layers of sandbags, usually laid with their long edge perpendicular to the trench. Rain and the coming and going of personnel soon smoothed out the parapets, blending them into the surrounding ground. The trenches were not zigzagged or dug to any geometric pattern; rather they could more accurately be described as "winding." At 30–50ft intervals shelters were erected to provide instant access to cover from enemy barrages. These shelters were constructed by building a three-sandbag-high, three-sandbag-thick wall on the trench front. A speed pallet or runway matting panels[9] were laid over the trench, sloping towards the rear, and two or three layers of sandbags stacked on top. Sometimes a firing port was provided.

DROP ZONE

L/3/26

L/3/26

33

30

27

RED SECTOR

32

31

28

24

23

19

18

ROCK QUARRY

26

29

25

22

20

21

15

14

16

13

FOB-3

TA CON VILLAGE

34

B/1/26

GRAY SECTOR

TO QL9

LEGEND

1 40mm/.50-cal position
2 ASP No. 1
3 C/1/13 Marines (105mm)
4 1/26 Marines COC
5 USAF Forward Operating Location
6 Reconnaissance units
7 Airfield control tower
8 Base Exchange and Post Office
9 26th Marines COC
10 Garbage dump
11 Additional helicopter parking
12 301st Seabees
13 Logistics Support Unit
14 Charlie Med
15 Graves registration
16 Aircraft parking area
17 Water point
18 Helicopter revetments
19 Air freight
20 Motor pool
21 ASP No. 2
22 Ponderosa (old Khe Sanh SF camp)
23 3d Engineer elements
24 A/1/13 Marines (105mm)
25 Mortar/1/13 Marines (4.2in)
26 FOB-3 command bunker
27 Tank and Ontos laager
28 1st Prov Battery (155mm)
29 1/13 Marines CP
30 H&S Co, 3/26 Marines
31 3/16 Marines COC
32 FOB-3 helicopter LZ
33 40mm/.50-cal position
34 3d Plat, Co O, CAP

KHE SANH COMBAT BASE, EARLY FEBRUARY 1968

KSCB's key facilities, defense sectors, perimeter defense and tenant units are indicated on the view of the base during the early phase of the siege. Unit locations remained static throughout the siege.

Note: Gridlines are marked at 250m/273yds

C/1/26

17

BLUE SECTOR

1

7

8

6

4

5

A/1/26

B/1/26

2

37TH RGR BTN

3

1

Fighting bunkers were more robustly constructed; an 8 x 8ft pit was dug and the interior sometimes revetted with sandbags. The walls above ground were typically three sandbags thick. If the fighting bunker was one of those protecting the perimeter, a firing port was built in. To provide additional support, timbers (6 x 6in) were placed in each corner, with a fifth in the center. A speed pallet or runway matting served as the roof, with two or three layers of sandbags stacked on top. This sort of bunker provided basic protection from 82mm mortars. U-shaped barbed-wire picket posts were often used as horizontal roof supports, and layers of packed earth and additional layers of sandbags were added along with plastic sheeting to provide a degree of water-proofing. Used 105mm howitzer and 106mm recoilless rifle cartridges were driven into the earth and into sandbag cover overhead with their rims touching, in order to detonate shells before they penetrated the bunker. Engineers with power tools could construct a bunker like this in three or four days; infantrymen needed a couple of days more.

Combat operations centers, fire-control centers, and other key facilities were housed in bunkers with at least twice the normal thickness of overhead cover. They would, nevertheless, often be destroyed if the enemy scored a direct hit with a 120mm mortar, 122mm rocket, 130mm or 152mm gun, particularly if the ordnance was fitted with a delay fuse. Some key bunkers had an additional outer blast wall, three-sandbag-thick, built a couple of feet from the bunker wall itself. Slit trenches were sometimes dug inside the bunker as additional protection should the bunker collapse – a common occurrence. Wooden ammunition boxes were filled with earth and stacked as revetments. Black fiberboard ammunition packing tubes and steel 155mm propellant bag tubes were also filled with earth and used as revetments, held in place by barbed-wire pickets, while 55-gallon fuel drums, again filled with earth, served as bunker walls. Some tents and wood-frame barracks had been erected previously, the latter roofed with corrugated sheet metal, but these were mostly destroyed and their materials salvaged. Building materials were sometimes in such short supply that guards had to be posted at night to prevent pilfering.

Critics complained that the Marines at Khe Sanh failed to entrench with sufficient thoroughness, blaming this deficiency on their normal role as assault troops and a natural aversion to defensive operations. Although this was undoubtedly true to a degree, this judgment was largely based on the observations of reporters who visited the base prior to the siege and during the build-up. The original garrison was a single battalion and the fortifications reflected this. More units poured in during the build-up but it took time to construct their positions, a situation often exacerbated by the slow arrival of materials, with ammunition and rations taking priority. Lumber in particular was in short supply and attempts to cut down local trees proved futile as they were so peppered by fragments from earlier fighting they damaged the chainsaws. C4 plastic explosive was used to fell trees to clear fields of fire and these were used for bunker materials, but there was a limit on how much C4 could be expended in this way. The wood had not been seasoned, and as such rotted quickly and fell prey to termites. The Marines dug feverishly and continued to improve positions during the siege, with deeper trenches and thicker overhead cover.

A more vertical view of KSCB providing a better view of its west end, though part of the Red Sector is cut off at the top of the photograph. FOB-3 compound is in the upper left. The KC-130F wreck of February 10 can be seen just below the west turnaround pad. Snaking out from the central portion of the north Gray Sector perimeter is the water point road. The dark area is the brush-covered stream gorge.

A typical hill position was 881S, occupied by elements of 3/26 for 113 days from December 26, 1967. Hill 881S was a dome-shaped hill with two peaks, the easternmost slightly higher than the west, the ridge fingers jutting out from the hillside. An oval perimeter trench encircled both peaks, with the area around the eastern hilltop being larger and more elongated. The hill had five helicopter landing zones (LZ) scattered across it. The eastern portion of the perimeter was defended by I/3/26 with three 105mm howitzers, two 81mm and three 60mm mortars, and contained the main ammunition bunkers. M/3/26 defended the west peak with two 106mm recoilless rifles and three 60mm mortars. I/3/26 commander, Capt William H. Dabney, had overall command of both companies. M60 and .50-cal machine-gun bunkers dotted the perimeter. On the saddle between the peaks was another LZ, and trenches linked the defended areas on both peaks. The hill trenches often had to be heavily strengthened with sandbags owing to the less stable condition of the soil. Troops dug slit trenches into the back wall of existing trenches, covering these "bunny holes" with airfield matting and sandbags, and 55gal drums with their ends cut out were laid end to end in ditches running downhill to provide drainage, as regular culvert piping was not available. A belt of concertina wire and mines surrounded the entire position. Wire repairs and the laying of mines and trip flares continued constantly. An access trail led west, down the slope out of the western perimeter. The slopes of the hill had been blasted clean of vegetation. Some 40 Marines would die on 881S, and over 150 more fall victim to wounds during the course of the siege; this despite the hill position never being the target of a ground attack. Nominally defended by 400 troops, the garrison sometimes fell as low as 250 because of the slow replacement rate. As the Marines themselves put it, there were two ways to get off the hill: "You're either flown off or blown off." Another example of the firepower of a Marine position is Hill 861, which had two 4.2in, two 81mm, and three 60mm mortars, plus a 106mm recoilless rifle.

Khe Sanh Combat Base had an elongated, irregularly shaped, trenched perimeter ("trenchway highway"), oriented east-southeast to west-northwest. It was some 2,500 yards long, averaging 400 yards wide, with the west end 650 yards across, occupying 2 square miles. The 3,895ft-long, 60ft-wide runway ran parallel with the north perimeter, situated less than 100 yards inside it and, on its eastern end, stretching some 150 yards beyond the perimeter. This narrow gap was covered by machine guns, Claymores, two Ontos vehicles loaded with flechette rounds, and pre-registered mortar concentrations, while booby-trapped concertina coils were strung at night. A turnaround pad was situated at both ends of the runway and a 150 x 600ft parking area was located south of the runway near the east end. Six soil-filled, steel-faced helicopter revetments were located on the other side of the runway from the parking area. When damaged by shell or mortar fire, the runway's aluminum AM2 matting was quickly repaired, with the damaged panels removed (some were salvaged for use in fortifications), the crater backfilled with packed earth and rock, and replacement panels laid.

The perimeter was divided into three sectors, thinly defended by 1/26 Marines. Blue Sector paralleled the runway's north side. Red Sector ran around the bulbous west end of the base, with FOB-3 linked in to the east. Gray Sector ran from behind FOB-3 along the south side and curved around the east end. The 150 x 650 yard FOB-3 compound was more heavily bunkered than the rest of KSCB and had its own helicopter LZ. The 37th ARVN Ranger Battalion occupied an outer perimeter at the east and southeast ends of KSCB. The west and east ends were considered the most likely points of attack and 1/9 Marines was dug in at the Rock Quarry 550 yards beyond the main perimeter's west end. References often depict this as a large kidney-shaped position extending over half a mile to the southwest with an outpost on Hill 64[10]. Instead it was a small cluster of interlinked positions and outposts around the quarry. The Hill 64 outpost was later withdrawn. The 200 x 300 yard drop zone (DZ) was situated between the main perimeter and 1/9 Marines. This location protected the DZ and allowed airdropped supplies to be recovered easily. The accuracy of the drops and the secure nature of the DZ avoided the problems with recovery of supplies experienced at Dien Bien Phu. The few supplies that were dropped outside the secure DZ were often recovered, but mortars and air power destroyed those that were not.

Khe Sanh's sole source of water was from an unnamed stream running parallel with and 150 yards outside the north perimeter. Water was pumped 800ft up an incline to rubber reservoirs beside the runway, and then to a small water tower. When the pumps failed or the reservoirs were under repair, water details using M76 Otter tracked carriers hauled 5gal water cans back to the base.

---

1 The French lost 11 x 120mm, 2 x 105mm, and 1 x 155mm weapons in the first two days.
2 Includes rounds fired on hill outposts.
3 Viet Minh claim they fired 350,000 rounds.
4 Most hills were identified by their elevation in meters above sea level.
5 Montagnard is the French term for "mountaineer," and referred to the planter/gatherer tribesmen of the Bru tribe indigenous to the uplands of Indochina. They lacked a written language and the Vietnamese referred to them as Moi ("savages").
6 The 12-man A-team was the basic Special Forces operating element employed to organize and train battalion-size indigenous Civilian Irregular Defense Group (CIDG) Camp Strike Forces.
7 West German-designed razor wire was made of galvanized spring steel with double-pointed, razor-like barbs. A coil was 40in in diameter and stretched out to approximately 50ft. The older spring steel concertina with twisted barbs remained in use.
8 These were half a 55gal steel drum buried in the ground at an angle, filled with jellied gasoline, with the top sealed. They were command-detonated by a Claymore firing device. A C4 charge blew the fuel 20 or more yards outward and it was ignited by a thermite grenade wired into the electrical firing system.
9 The 463-L speed pallets measured 8 x 9ft and AM2 matting panels 2 x 12ft. The M8 pierced steel planking from the old runway was left on the base and the planks, measuring 1 x 12ft, were also used.
10 In this case its name was not based on its elevation.

CHRONOLOGY

PRE-1967

July 1962 Special Forces camp established at Khe Sanh.
April 1964 Marine Signal Engineering Survey Unit conducts communications intelligence collection in area.
April 1966 1/1 Marines conducts Operation *Virginia* in Khe Sanh area, yielding few results.
October 1966 1/3 Marines commences operations in Khe Sanh area.
December 21, 1966 Khe Sanh Special Forces camp relocates to Lang Vei.

1967

March 19 QL9 opened between Dong Ha and Khe Sanh.
April 20 3d Marines commences Operation *Prairie IV* in Khe Sanh area.
April 24 Contacts with NVA north of Hill 861 and the Hill Battles commence.
April 28 2/3 Marines seizes Hill 861.
May 2 2/3 Marines seizes Hill 881S.
May 4 NVA attacks Lang Vei Special Forces Camp.
May 5 2/3 Marines seizes Hill 881N.
May 13 Hill Battles are terminated. 1/26 Marines occupies KSCB, Hills 881S, 861, and 950. Operation *Crockett* commences.
July 16 Operation *Crockett* terminated.
July 17 Operation *Ardmore* commences with little action.
August 17 Khe Sanh airfield closed for restoration and expansion.
mid August QL9 cut by NVA.
September 2 3/26 Marines departs KSCB.
September 27 New Lang Vei Special Forces Camp opened closer to Laotian border.
October 27 Khe Sanh airfield re-opened.
October 31 Operation *Ardmore* terminated.
November 1 Operation *Scotland I* commences.
December 13 3/26 Marines returns to KSCB.
December 21 Evidence of NVA build-up found in Khe Sanh area.

1968

January 2 At least two NVA divisions in Khe Sanh area.
January 15 Operation *Niagara* commences to provide massive air support to KSCB.
January 16–17 2/26 Marines arrives at KSCB and occupies Hill 558.
January 20 KSCB placed on Red Alert due to pending major NVA attack.
January 20/21 NVA conducts major assault on Hill 861. NVA commences operations to ensure QL9 remains cut.
January 21 Massive NVA artillery, rocket, and mortar attack on KSCB destroys ASP 1. Khe Sanh village seized by NVA.
January 22–23 1/9 Marines arrives and takes position in Rock Quarry west of KSCB.
January 23–28 Large numbers of refugees are evacuated from KSCB by air.
January 27 37th ARVN Ranger Battalion arrives at KSCB.
January 30/31 Communists launch nationwide Tet Offensive. First B-52 strike delivered at Khe Sanh.
February 1–25 The battle for Hue, one of the key cities in northern South Vietnam.
February 5 Elements of 2/26 secure Hill 861A. The NVA conducts major assault on the position.
February 7 Lang Vei Special Forces Camp falls to a combined tank/infantry assault by NVA units.

February 8 The outpost west of the Rock Quarry is almost overrun and is withdrawn.

February 10 KC-130F crash-lands at KSCB and C-130 landings are suspended on the 12th. Airdrop and low-altitude parachute extractions (LAPES) become the base's primary means of resupply.

February 21 NVA units probe 37th Ranger Battalion lines.

February 23 The heaviest day of shelling at KSCB: 1,307 rounds strike the base.

February 25 A Marines patrol ambushed south of KSCB suffers heavy losses.

February 29–April 1 NVA regiment attempts to position itself to attack 37th Ranger Battalion.

March 6 C-123 transport aircraft shot down approaching KSCB.

March 7 Large numbers of refugees evacuated from KSCB by air.

March 10 Provisional Corps, Vietnam established, subordinate to III MAF and responsible for Operation *Pegasus*.

March 23 Heaviest day of shelling for March: 1,109 rounds.

March 25 Preliminary reconnaissance by 1st CavDiv for Operation *Pegasus* begins.

March 31 Operations *Scotland I* and *Niagara* terminated.

April 1 Operation *Pegasus* commences with 1st CavDiv, 1st Marines, and ARVN units.

April 4 2/5 Cavalry secures Old French Fort and Khe Sanh village.

April 5 1/9 Marines repulses NVA counterattack on Hill 471.

April 6 2/12 Cavalry relieves 1/9 Marines on Hill 471.

April 8 2/7 Cavalry links up with 26th Marines, officially lifting the siege.

April 9 US troops secure Lang Vei. Khe Sanh airfield declared open to all aircraft.

April 11 QL9 is officially opened to Khe Sanh. 37th Ranger Battalion departs.

April 14 3/26 seizes Hill 881N.

April 15 Operation *Pegasus* is terminated. Operation *Scotland II* commences with 3d Marines (terminated February 28, 1969).

April 18 26th Marines deployed to Quang Tri City and Dong Ha.

May 13 Peace talks between the US, South Vietnam and North Vietnam commence in Paris.

June 19 Elements of the 1st and 9th Marines begin Operation *Charlie*, the dismantling and evacuation of KSCB.

July 5 KSCB officially closed.

July 6 KSCB evacuated and Operation *Charlie* completed.

July 11 Last action in the Khe Sanh area when 1/1 Marines engages NVA near Hill 689.

PRELUDE

THE HILL BATTLES, APRIL–MAY 1967

The siege of Khe Sanh Combat Base was not the first battle fought between the NVA and the US and ARVN allies on the Khe Sanh plateau. With the realization that Free World military operations and pacification efforts in the northern provinces were gradually eroding their previously hard-won footholds in the region, the NVA decided to attack the exposed and lightly defended base in an effort to reverse this trend. The communist infrastructure that had been so carefully and painstakingly established was unraveling in many areas. The NVA began to build up its strength in areas north of the DMZ and in Laos in mid 1966, an initiative that would eventually draw steadily more American and ARVN units away from the population centers of South Vietnam to the border regions, requiring Free World forces to spread themselves more thinly.

In April 1967 Khe Sanh was the most northwest outpost of Free World forces in South Vietnam. It was undeveloped, possessing only an airstrip, and a variety of Free World units were scattered across the plateau. These included a Special Forces camp at Lang Vei manned by Civilian Irregular Defense Group (CIDG) troops, a Regional Force company and a Marine Combined Action Program (CAP) company at Khe Sanh village, a Marine battalion at the airfield, and an MACV-SOG FOB at the Old French Fort outside Khe Sanh village. QL9 had been re-opened by the Marine 11th Engineer Battalion on March 19, but this road link was tenuous.

The perimeter bunker line connected by trenches. Some of these are fighting bunkers, some living bunkers, and others are a combination. Most have at least three-sandbag-thick overhead cover, which provided sufficient protection from 60mm and 82mm mortars.

Map labels (top to bottom, left to right):

325th

HILL 881N

2

HILL

N

A

C

HILL 861*

3

HILL 881S*

1

HILL 758

HILL

HILL 684

HILL 64 (AKA 564)*

D

304th

HILL 552

NORTH VIETNAMESE ARMY UNITS AND EVENTS

A 4 Battalion, 95C Regiment attempts to seize Hill 861 during 20/21 January assault and is repulsed by K/3/26 Marines and elements of A/1/26 and D/1/26.

B Unidentified NVA platoon probes west perimeter 21 January and is repulsed by L/3/26 Marines.

C Unidentified battalion, 325C Division attempts to seize Hill 861A during 6 February assault, which partly overruns the position, but is repulsed by E/2/26 Marines.

D Unidentified battalion, 101C Regiment attempts to seize Hill 64 (Outpost Alpha 1) during 8 February assault and is barely repulsed by 1st Platoon, A/1/9 Marines. The outpost is abandoned the next day.

E Unidentified NVA company probes east perimeter on 21 February and is repulsed by the 37th ARVN Ranger Battalion.

F Unidentified battalion, 66 Regiment attempts to assault the east perimeter on 1 March and is repulsed by the Rangers (seven subsequent light probes are conducted in following weeks).

G Unidentified battalion, 66 Regiment attempts to assault the east perimeter on 18 March and is repulsed by the Rangers.

US MARINE CORPS UNITS AND EVENTS

* Indicates US position. (squares 1-8)

1 Hill 881S defended by I/3/26 Marines plus two platoons and M/3/26 Command Group.

2 I/3/26 Marines attempts two-prong attack on Hill 881N, 20 January, and is repulsed. This was the only significant Marine offensive operation during the siege.

3 Hill 861 defended by K/3/26 Marines plus two platoons A/1/26, and one platoon D/1/26.

4 Hill 861A defended E/2/26 Marines, which occupied it on 5 February.

5 Hill 558 defended by 2/26 Marines (- E/2/26).

6 Hill 950 radio relay site defended by 2d Platoon, A/1/26 Marines.

7 Rock Quarry defended by 1/9 Marines, which occupied it on 23 January.

8 Hill 64 defended by 1st Platoon, A/1/9 Marines, which occupied it on 23 January until withdrawn on 8 February after a heavy attack.

BATTLE FOR THE HILLS, LATE JANUARY–EARLY FEBRUARY, 1968

Most action in the vicinity of KSCB focused on the Marine outpost hills to the north of the base.

Note: Gridlines are shown at intervals of 1km/0.62 miles

The blue outlined boxes are B-52 Arc Light bombing areas.
Arc Lights could be delivered in other areas with prior coordination.

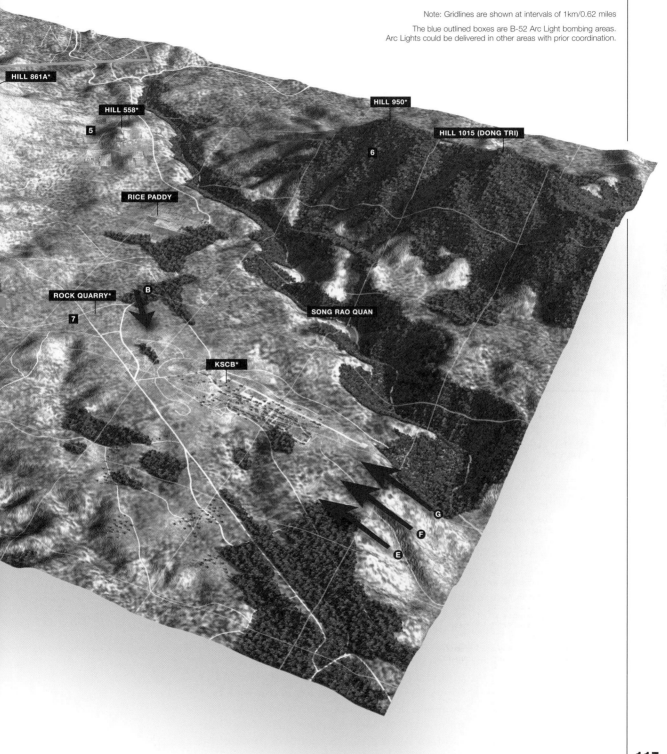

HILL 861A*

HILL 558*

5

HILL 950*

HILL 1015 (DONG TRI)

6

RICE PADDY

ROCK QUARRY*

B

SONG RAO QUAN

7

KSCB*

G

F

E

With the American flag flying defiantly above it, what appears to be a heap of discarded ammunition tubes and 55gal drums is actually the combat operations center for I/3/26 Marines on Hill 881S. The 4.2in mortar ammunition tubes are earth-filled and serve as bullet and fragmentation deflectors for personnel entering and exiting the underground bunker. Barbed-wire pickets hold the stacked tubes in place, but appear to have taken some mortar hits.

1st Battalion, 3d Marines (1/3) had deployed to the area at the end of September 1966 to conduct Operation *Prairie*. It patrolled out as far as 6,500 yards from the airfield, very slightly more than the maximum range of NVA 120mm mortars. Patrols were soon extended to 11,000 yards. Operation *Prairie* was wound down at the end of January 1967, having produced few contacts with the enemy. 1/3 Marines departed and a reinforced Company B, 1st Battalion, 9th Marines (B/1/9) garrisoned the airfield with the artillery of Battery I/3/12 Marines. NVA activity began to increase in the area in late February and continued to do so into March. A misdirected air strike struck Khe Sanh village in early March, and this "friendly fire" killed over 100 civilians and wounded over 200. The Marines did conduct relief efforts in the aftermath of this tragedy. At the same time the NVA units mortared the airfield, damaging helicopters. They also probed the defenses around the base. The 3d MarDiv, responsible for northern I CTZ, reinforced Khe Sanh with E/2/9 and stepped up patrolling.

On March 16 a major firefight took place, resulting in 19 Marines KIA and 59 WIA, and some helicopter losses. In response two tanks, three Ontos, two quad .50-cal vehicles, and two twin 40mm "Dusters" were sent to Khe Sanh. E/2/9 Marines, which had suffered most of the losses, was withdrawn and Battery F/2/12 replaced I/3/12. The 3d Marines (Col John P. Lanigan), operating to the east of Khe Sanh, was made responsible for the area in which fewer than 1,000 US and Vietnamese troops were operating at that point. B/1/9, conducting a sweep on April 24, was involved in a minor engagement on Hill 861, beginning what came to be known as the Hill Battles or First Battle of Khe Sanh. The first day's action cost the Marines 14 KIA and 17 WIA, strongly indicating that the NVA were marshalling forces to overrun the lightly defended Khe Sanh, in order to win a combined military and propaganda victory.

The NVA plan was to isolate the base, destroy the helicopters based there, cut QL9 and conduct diversionary attacks on Marine bases to the east and Lang Vei Special Forces Camp. The 18 NVA Regiment, attached to 325C Division, would attack KSCB from the northwest. The diversionary attacks on Camp Carroll, Con Thien, Dong Ha, Gio Linh, and Phu Bai were carried out on April 27–28 as planned, despite the enemy plan having been compromised.

Infantrymen of G/2/3 Marines work their way up the blasted south slopes of 881S during the April–May 1967 Hill Battles.

K/3/3 was helicoptered into Khe Sanh on April 25 and advanced on Hill 861 to join B/1/9 in clearing the feature. The 3/3 Command Group (LtCol Gary Wilder) was in charge of the operation. The terrain was difficult and resistance strong, and K/3/9 was choppered into KSCB as reinforcement. On the morning of the 26th, 3/3 Combat Operations Center (COC) and KSCB were struck by heavy mortar attacks and the NVA occupied Hill 881S in strength. Fighting continued all day on Hill 861, with close-range ambushes initiated by the NVA, and the three Marine companies withdrew at nightfall. In a glimpse of what the future would hold, US and ARVN action was hampered by dense vegetation, fog, and heavy rains.

Realizing that 3/3 was facing a large force scattered over a wide area, 3d MarDiv committed 2/3 Marines (LtCol Earl R. DeLong), which was conducting operations on the coast north of Hue. The battalion was airlifted to Khe Sanh on the afternoon of the 26th and immediately deployed into the hills. The next day 3/3 pulled back to the base to receive replacements and resupply, and 2/3's fourth company arrived along with artillery reinforcement. Air power and artillery, including 175mm guns firing from the Rockpile, softened up Hill 861 throughout April 28. Marine fighters slammed 250lb and 500lb bombs into Hill 861 to blast away foliage. With the stoutly built NVA bunkers now exposed, they were attacked individually with 750lb, 1,000lb, and 2,000lb bombs.

The 3d Marines launched its assault in the afternoon of April 28 with Hill 861 as Objective 1, 881S Objective 2, and 881N Objective 3. Leading off was 3/2, which ascended Hill 861 to find the NVA had withdrawn. On the bare hilltop the Marines found 25 bunkers and 400 foxholes, and 3/3 prepared to take 881S the next day. The going the next morning was slow, but before noon Marine elements were in contact with NVA patrols. The battalion's intermediate objective, a small hill mass 750m northeast of 881S, was secured before nightfall. The night was uneventful as 881S was pounded with artillery and air strikes.

On the morning of April 30, 3/3 moved out toward 881S while 3/2 departed 861 to secure an attack position to the west of 881S. Soon 3/2 was engaging a bunker complex and was forced to pull back; 3/3 was

The Hill Fights. Though large areas were blasted almost clear of the dense vegetation, the fallen trees and tangled limbs coupled with the naturally rugged hillsides and cratered ground made cross-country movement extremely difficult.

also heavily engaged and pulled back. It was now apparent that 881S was very heavily defended. The battalions suffered a combined total of 52 KIA and 152 WIA, but enemy losses were at least three times higher. On May 1, 881S and 881N were plastered with massive aerial and artillery barrages. M/3/3 had suffered so many casualties it was flown back to Dong Ha. Some 106mm recoilless rifles were brought forward to engage the bunkers with direct-fire, and 3/3 assaulted 881S on the morning of May 2, securing the hill in the early afternoon. It had been abandoned by the NVA. They found 250 bunkers, of which 200 had been destroyed by air strikes and artillery. Sometime around May 1, the battered NVA 18 Regiment was replaced by the fresh 95C Regiment, 325C Division.

Since April 28, 2/3 had been clearing the area northwest of Hill 861 in preparation for the 881N assault. Moving out on the morning of May 2, the hill was assaulted from the south and east in the late morning. Using artillery support, the crest was gained, but a sudden heavy rainstorm and high winds made effective control of the position impossible, and the Marines were forced to pull back to defendable terrain for the night. Before dawn on May 3, as the Marines prepared to again assault 881N, the NVA hit them with a counterattack. The position held by E/2/3, on a small hill 500m south of 881N, was penetrated and a vicious hand-to-hand fight ensued. The penetration was contained by dawn, and the rest of the day was spent clearing the enemy lodgment, further delaying the 881N attack. The Marines lost 27 dead and 84 wounded, but 137 NVA dead were left in the area.

It was learned from the three prisoners that were taken that another attack was planned for the night of May 3. The battalion closed into a tight perimeter on the south slope of 881N. Wire, Claymores, and trip flares were flown in and the battalion waited. Instead of the NVA attacking 881N, they struck the Lang Vei Special Forces Camp 10km to the south in the early hours of May 4. This attack had been planned by the NVA as a diversion for a larger attack on Khe Sanh. Even though the Marine actions in the hills had undermined the main attack, the Lang Vei assault was launched anyway. It had no impact on the Hill Battles, but showed that the NVA was more widely deployed in the area than had been realized. The camp was almost overrun, but held out. Two US Special Forces (USSF) were killed along with 20 CIDG, with another 37 CIDG either captured or deserted. The 2/3 spent May 4 moving further up 881N as the hill was prepared for an assault by air strikes and artillery. The assault was finally launched on the morning of May 5. Encountering heavy resistance, the battalion pulled back and again blasted the hill. This forced the NVA to withdraw and the hilltop was secured by mid-afternoon.

For the next three days there was little contact with the NVA as both battalions patrolled the area. Aerial observers reported enemy elements withdrawing north and west. Patrolling continued and efforts were made to pursue enemy rearguards. On May 9 a two-platoon patrol engaged an enemy force. The patrol was beyond radio range, but its fire requests were relayed through another unit. Helicopters flew in mortars and recoilless rifles and helicopter gunships hit the enemy, turning the NVA withdrawal into a rout. The Marines lost 24 KIA and 19 WIA, however. The last action of the Hill Battles was on May 10 when a 3d Reconnaissance Battalion patrol was engaged and extracted with great difficulty.

Helicopter support as well as fixed-wing transports were critical to sustaining Khe Sanh and the hill positions during the siege. Here a Marine CH-46A Sea Knight, or "Purple Fox" medium cargo helicopter lifts off from Khe Sanh to deliver a sling-load of ammunition to one of the hill positions.

While the Hill Battles were only company- and battalion-sized actions, it had been a tough fight. The Marines suffered 155 KIA and 425 WIA, and lost a number of helicopters. These losses were significant enough that some companies were withdrawn during the action and rebuilt. Marine Aviation delivered 1,900 tons of ordnance and the artillery over 25,000 rounds, while B-52s flew 23 strikes against the surrounding area. The Hill Battles were the first major actions in which the Marines used the 5.56mm M16 rifle, which had replaced the 7.62mm M14. There were widespread problems with the weapon jamming, caused both by improper cleaning and defects in the weapon's design, which were later corrected.

The planned NVA attack on KSCB had been foiled and the body count confirmed that it had lost at least 940 dead (total losses may have been as high as 1,500). It would be almost six months before 325C NVA Division was again ready for major operations.

Marine forces in the Khe Sanh area were scaled down beginning on May 11, and on May 13 the 26th Marines (Forward), under Colonel John J. Padley, relieved the 3d Marines at KSCB and Operation *Crockett* began. Only 1/26 Marines was present with a small regimental command group on the base. A company fortified Hill 861 and Hill 881S, with a platoon securing the radio relay site on Hill 950. Patrols were conducted to a distance of 4,300 yards from the positions, while Company A, 3d Reconnaissance Battalion, patrolled further out. Contacts indicated elements of 325C Division were still in the tri-border region. June saw increasing enemy probes and mortar and rocket attacks. One engagement west of 881S on June 6 cost the Marines 18 dead and 28 wounded, while NVA losses were at least 66 confirmed KIA. Because of increasing enemy activity, 3/26 Marines arrived on June 13. Early on the morning of June 27 two mortar and rocket attacks on KSCB left ten dead and 139 wounded. Activity petered out and Operation *Crockett* was terminated on July 16 with 52 Marine KIA and 255 WIA. NVA losses were over 200 confirmed dead.

On July 17 Operation *Ardmore* began, but there were few contacts and the operation was ended on October 31. During this period Marine and NVA losses were relatively light at ten and 100 respectively. From mid-August to late October the Khe Sanh airfield was closed while it was refurbished and extended by Naval Mobile Construction Battalion 10; this was just at the point that the NVA managed once again to cut QL9. Colonel David E. Lownds took command of the 26th Marines on August 12, and on September 2 3/26 Marines departed the area. At the end of September the Lang Vei Special Forces Camp was relocated closer to the Laotian border. November 1 saw the start of Operation *Scotland I*, the defense of the Khe Sanh area. On December 13, 3/26 Marines returned to KSCB as a response to renewed NVA activity.

OPPOSING PLANS

THE NORTH VIETNAMESE PLAN

In April 1967 the North Vietnamese Politburo and Central Military Party Committee conducted assessments of the feasibility of launching a major campaign to achieve a decisive victory in South Vietnam. The decision was made in June to execute what would become the Tet Offensive[11]. The plan called for widespread attacks throughout the country focusing on urban areas, which they considered the enemy's weakest points. Preparations were made by sending cadres south to coordinate the operation with NVA and VC units and, by October, supplies had been stockpiled along the Ho Chi Minh Trail using over 5,000 trucks. Additional units, including sappers, were sent south along with new weapons. Plans were firmed up in October, at the same time that additional US units began deploying to Vietnam, and the final go-ahead was given in January 1968, just before the planned launch date. In late December, however, the US became aware of the build-up of forces in the Khe Sanh area. This did not deter NVA plans and indeed may have been part of the preparations for Tet, aimed at drawing troops away from the urban centers.

The US command interpreted the increasing movement of NVA units and supplies into Quang Tri as an effort to create another Dien Bien Phu at Khe Sanh. The deception worked in the NVA's favor as the US focused on remote northwestern Quang Tri, allowing NVA units to move into position near Dong Ha, Hue, and other Tet Offensive targets more easily. The four NVA divisions, and considerable additional forces, committed to Quang Tri had the mission of tying down as many Free World forces as possible in what was envisioned as a General Offensive-General Uprising (*Tong Kong Kich-Tong Khoi Nghia*). It has since been postulated that the General Uprising was as much as anything an effort by the North

Absolutely essential to the defense of Khe Sanh was close air support provided by a variety of Marine, Navy, and Air Force fighter-bombers. Here a Marine Grumman A-6A Intruder and McDonnell-Douglas F-4B Phantom II head for an air strike. Fully loaded, these two aircraft alone could each carry more 500lb bombs than four World War II B-17 bombers.

Vietnamese to eliminate the VC as a political/military force in its own right within South Vietnam. This result would enable North Vietnam to avoid dealing with an independent South Vietnamese nationalist movement once victory was achieved. Previous battles had taught the NVA that the US Forces' superior firepower and mobility meant it could not win a conventional engagement. This was confirmed in mid 1967 by the battles for Dak To, Song Ba, and Loc Ninh. In response, the NVA switched many of its Tet targets from US to ARVN units.

On the night of January 20, elements of, from west to east, 304, 325C, and 320 Divisions would conduct attacks to ensure the road route to Khe Sanh along QL9 remained closed. The 325C Division would conduct operations to the northwest and north of Khe Sanh, although its 95C Regiment and 8 Battalion, 29C Regiment, were deployed to the east. The 304 Division was to the southwest and south, while 320 was in support, with most elements north of the Rockpile to the northeast of Khe Sanh, and 324B further north in the DMZ as a reserve. The first attack on KSCB's hill position would take place at the same time. The following day (January 21) would see the opening artillery barrages on Khe Sanh.

The actual intentions of the NVA in northwestern Quang Tri remain unknown. Even *Victory in Vietnam: The Official History of the People's Army of Vietnam, 1954–1975* fails to provide any insight into their objectives. Nguyen Van Mai of the Politburo stated, "We will entice the Americans close to the border and bleed them without mercy." It is suspected, because operations there began ten days prior to the launch of the Tet Offensive, that their primary goal was to draw in forces and tie them down both at Khe Sanh and in efforts to re-open QL9. While significant US air and logistical resources were required to support Khe Sanh, no effort was made to open QL9 until after the Tet Offensive had been blunted.

Even less is known of the actual designs on KSCB, which the NVA called Ta Con after the nearest Montagnard village. Was the plan actually to overrun the base, winning a tremendous political and psychological victory that would have the same resounding effects as the triumph at Dien Bien Phu? Or was it merely to surround the base and draw and hold Free World forces there? Hindsight suggests the most likely scenario is the latter. Two woefully under-strength divisions, enduring a constant pounding from Free World forces, were hardly adequate to carry the base.

The NVA were focused on mobile combat (*danh van dong*) and the idea of siege warfare was just as distasteful to them as defensive warfare was to the Marines. Trenches were dug toward the base's east end and south side, however, beginning in mid February. This was perhaps to strengthen the impression of an impending assault. Numbers of 60mm[12] and 82mm mortars were moved within range of the base and well dug in and concealed. A 12.7mm antiaircraft machine gun platoon protected each mortar platoon. Troop positions and supply dumps scattered through the hills were thoroughly dug in and in some cases suffered less damage than expected from air and artillery.

If the NVA's intention was an assault to overrun the base, it missed its best chance in the period January 20–22, when the main ammunition dump had been destroyed, the runway damaged, before the hill positions were fully developed, before 1/9 Marines was fully dug in at the Rock Quarry, and before the 37th ARVN Ranger Battalion arrived.

Hindsight is a marvelous thing, but nonetheless NVA efforts to assault the base did seem feeble. Only two significant attacks were conducted on hill outposts during the entire siege, both of which came close to success: Hill 861 on January 20 and 861A on February 5. It is often said that American firepower prevented the NVA from conducting a major assault, but at this early stage the full weight of that firepower had not yet been brought to bear and the NVA was not as yet overly affected by it. If 861 had been seized early on, it is possible that the NVA would have made a more serious attempt to attack the base. Why it did not make a serious attempt on 861 is unknown, but does suggest that their aims may have fallen short of the actual capture of the base.

Of particular interest is that the NVA made no effort to destroy Khe Sanh's reservoirs or contaminate the base's water supply, the source of which was in NVA-controlled territory. If they had done so it would have been necessary for 258 tons of water to be delivered daily, exceeding the 235 tons of other daily cargo that was difficult enough to deliver. Just as puzzling is the fact that the NVA never cut the telephone line linking KSCB to the outside world, nor made serious efforts to destroy the radio relay site on Hill 950 protected by a solitary platoon. Nor were significant antiaircraft units moved into the area. There were large numbers of light antiaircraft weapons, but none larger than 37mm, and the concentration was not nearly as heavy as during the 1973 siege of An Loc. The numbers of US and South Vietnamese aircraft lost and heavily damaged were comparatively small. While Lang Vei Special Forces Camp and Khe Sanh village were overrun, the number of determined attacks on the outposts was small. Assault trenches were sapped to within 100 yards or less of the base's perimeter, but these were not nearly as numerous as those dug at Dien Bien Phu. The number of probes was limited and the only actual ground attacks on the main perimeter were conducted over a month after the siege commenced and fell far short of the expected human-wave attacks, being conducted by fewer than 100 men. If the NVA had been serious about taking the base they would surely have assaulted it as early as possible rather than wait and allow their manpower and ammunition to be whittled away.

The artillery, rocket, and mortar fire directed against Khe Sanh and the outposts was relatively light, averaging 150 rounds per day, barely exceeding 1,000 rounds even on the days of heaviest bombardment. Total expenditure amounted to just over 11,000 rounds, including 5,000 122mm rockets. At Dien Bien Phu the French were the target of over 2,000 rounds on many days, Corregidor received 16,000 rounds in a single day in WWII, and a tiny US hilltop outpost in Korea once took 14,000 rounds in a day. While artillery dominated the battlefield, the actual amount employed was probably not all that high.

While it appears there was no firm plan to overrun the base, no doubt the NVA were prepared to attempt to do so if the opportunity arose. The NVA intentions to overrun the base or otherwise certainly did not change what its defenders endured and were prepared for. It was a seemingly unending battle, 24 hours a day for 77 grueling, mind-numbing days. It was even worse for the NVA enduring constant artillery and aerial bombardment, the heaviest inflicted during the war. The logistical effort to sustain NVA forces was an even greater endeavor than the siege itself.

The first NVA use of armor in combat in South Vietnam took the form of PT-76 light amphibious tanks committed to the assault on Lang Vei. The Americans failed to interpret how these tanks would be employed. It was expected that they would be utilized in the assault on the main base and the Marines were well prepared for such an eventuality, being armed with 90mm gun tanks, 106mm recoilless rifles, 3.5in bazookas, M72 light antitank weapons (LAW), and antitank mines. However, the NVA had decided not to employ them against the main base because they would have been easy prey for the American tanks and Ontos antitank vehicles. Instead, they were first used against a Laotian battalion to drive them across the border, and then against Lang Vei Special Forces Camp.

The Tet Offensive had spent itself by the end of February, although NVA units were still in the process of disengaging. NVA units were first detected withdrawing from Khe Sanh on March 15, but this process probably began earlier. The withdrawal quickened as the relief forces drew steadily nearer to Khe Sanh, although the fighting was far from over. March 23 saw a heavy shelling of KSCB and there were still sharp engagements around the base, as well as opposition to the relief operation. Probes, patrol engagements, and shelling continued until the Americans evacuated Khe Sanh on July 6.

THE AMERICAN PLAN

Regardless of its exposed location, Gen William Westmoreland, US commander in Vietnam, desired to maintain a presence at Khe Sanh as a position from which to conduct operations against the Ho Chi Minh Trail and as a reconnaissance launch site. He felt it was essential to maintain an intelligence collection capability in the tri-border area. In December 1967 the Free World presence at Khe Sanh was limited, with only a reinforced Marine company backed by an artillery battery, a CIDG camp strike force at Lang Vei, a Regional Force company in Khe Sanh village, and a

Command and Control North (CCN) launch site in the form of FOB-3. To make matters worse, these small units were scattered over a wide area, making mutual support impossible. QL9 had been closed west of Ca Lu since August, leaving air power as the only means of reinforcement and resupply.

Because of its remoteness, unfavorable weather conditions, and proximity to NVA supply lines, Khe Sanh would be a difficult position to maintain. In 1966, III MAF conducted a map exercise of the defense of Quang Tri Province after which Westmoreland questioned why the defense plan had not included Khe Sanh. The Marines argued the remote area was not defensible, or at least not worth the logistical effort of doing so.

Another reason Khe Sanh was to be retained was for its eventual incorporation into the ill-conceived "Dyemarker" Strongpoint/Obstacle System, known to posterity as the "McNamara Line." This was planned as a line of barriers, mines, belts of cleared land, and remote sensors backed by artillery strongpoints and mobile forces. Its development and the construction of strongpoints had begun in 1967. Many military leaders felt all it achieved was to tie down units in static positions rather than allowing them to exploit their superior mobility. In addition the barrier could simply be outflanked through Laos, even though remote sensors were to "cover" that area.

When an NVA build-up was detected in December 1967, the Marines began to reinforce KSCB and continued to do so until shortly after the siege began. In preparation for increased operations there, and acknowledging the fact that QL9 was cut and would be extremely costly to re-open and maintain, Khe Sanh airfield had been renovated and extended in August and September. The monsoon began in October. Operation *Ardmore*, the defense of the Khe Sanh area, was terminated and Operation *Scotland I* began on November 1 with the same mission. Intelligence collection efforts in the area were increased as the weather deteriorated, using ground patrols, aerial reconnaissance, radio intercept, infrared aerial photography, and helicopter-borne "people sniffers."

Reinforcements were sent in once the decision was made to hold the base. External long-range artillery support was to be provided by Army

175mm guns at the Rockpile and Camp Carroll. Marine, Air Force, and Navy carrier aircraft would support the base and Air Force transports and Marine helicopters would supply it as part of Operation *Niagara*. Sufficient airlift was available to keep the base supplied, though more was requested: Boeing C-130E Hercules of the 315th Air Division, Fairchild C-123K Providers and De Havilland C-7A Caribous of the 834th Air Division, and Marine KC-130Fs. Weather, almost as significant a factor as NVA artillery, would be the deciding factor on the effectiveness of this air power.

Some urged that Khe Sanh be abandoned rather than allowing the Marines to become bogged down in a siege in a remote position difficult to supply and hampered by bad weather. The highest US authorities directed that Khe Sanh be held, however, "because it afforded an opportunity to draw large enemy forces to battle, then destroy them with a combination of superior firepower and a counterthrust into Laos." The counterthrust never took place. The similarity of this statement to the French concept of the defense of Dien Bien Phu further fueled the endless media comparisons of the two actions. Westmoreland said, "We will lure the enemy to their deaths," in a statement strikingly similar to Nguyen Van Mai's. The US understood early on that a large relief effort would be necessary to eventually open QL9. What was not realized at the time of the decision to hold Khe Sanh was that the Tet Offensive would delay that relief. The insistence on holding Khe Sanh, and undertaking whatever effort was necessary to ensure it would not fall, distracted American attention from other areas.

The Khe Sanh defense plan was simple and straightforward. This type of static warfare was repugnant to the Marines and most in the Marine chain-of-command disagreed with the concept, but Westmoreland prevailed. Being primarily an assault force, their mentality and doctrine called for aggressive offensive operations. A single Marine battalion and the many small support detachments defended KSCB itself. A single rifle company was held in reserve. The dug-in tanks and Ontos were concentrated at the base's west end during the day, but some would move to different perimeter sectors at night. A

The Marine commanders overseeing the defense of Khe Sanh, from left to right: MajGen Rathvon McC. Tompkins, Commanding General, 3d MarDiv; Gen Leonard F. Chapman, Commandant of the Marine Corps; MajGen Louis Metzger, Assistant Commander, 3d MarDiv; and LtGen Robert E. Cushman, Commanding General, III MAF. The occasion is MajGen Metzger's January 1968 promotion. Metzger's tour of duty was soon completed and he was replaced by BGen Jacob E. Glick (not pictured).

quad .50-cal and a Duster were positioned near each end of the base. An understrength ARVN Ranger battalion was dug in on the east end, the most likely direction of a ground assault. FOB-3 secured part of the south perimeter. Another Marine battalion was positioned outside the west end of the perimeter in the Rock Quarry, another likely direction of attack. It also secured the DZ. Lang Vei Special Forces Camp and light indigenous defenses at Khe Sanh village provided dubious protection of the southwest approach from Laos along QL9. Hills 881S, 861, and 950, a radio relay site, were already occupied by Marines. The hill outposts were considered essential to the defense. Hill 558 and the surrounding area were occupied just before the siege commenced in January. A composite artillery battalion was positioned on the base itself with three 105mm howitzers on 881S. Hill 881S and 861 denied the NVA rocket and artillery firing positions, while 558 blocked the approach through the Rao Qung gorge.

For the most part Marine patrols were restricted from straying further than 500 yards outside their perimeter because of the density of enemy troops and the difficulties of supporting and extracting them if they became strongly engaged further out. On the eve of the NVA attack 1st Brigade, 101st AbnDiv, and 3d Brigade, 1st CavDiv, were ordered to be prepared to deploy to I CTZ at 24 hours' notice and then to air-assault into Khe Sanh or an adjacent area. Both brigades were helicopter-borne airmobile units. Basically the defense plan was for the Marines simply to hold until relieved. Until Operation *Pegasus* began there was little in the way of maneuver by either side. Planning for this relief operation had originally been begun by the 1st CavDiv in late January, but its commitment to Hue and other operations countering the Tet Offensive operations delayed the relief's implementation.

---

11 Tet Nguyen Dan – Festival of the Lunar New Year beginning on January 30 in the South Vietnamese calendar and January 31 in the North Vietnamese calendar.
12 The Chinese 60mm was referred to by the US as the "61mm" based on the theory that, as with the Soviet/Chinese 82mm, US 81mm ammunition could not be fired from it. Both US and Chinese 60mms can in fact fire each other's ammunition.

OPPOSING COMMANDERS

AMERICAN COMMANDERS

Military Assistance Command, Vietnam, the senior US joint command in Vietnam, was directed by **Gen William C. Westmoreland**, a position he held from 1964 to 1968. For more direct control of operations in far away I CTZ during the Tet Offensive, MACV established a sub-headquarters, MACV Forward on February 9, 1968 at Phu Bai. **Gen Creighton W. Abrams**, Deputy Commander, MACV, had direct supervision over III MAF. On March 10, MACV Forward was dissolved and its assets used to form Provisional Corps, Vietnam, under **LtGen William B. Rosson**, former Deputy Commander, MACV Forward. Provisional Corps was subordinated to III MAF and made responsible for the relief of Khe Sanh. In August this command was consolidated with XXIV Corps newly arrived in Vietnam.

LtGen Robert E. Cushman, Jr. (USMC) was Commanding General, III MAF, responsible for US operations in I CTZ. He oversaw the defense and relief of Khe Sanh. Born in 1914, he graduated from the Naval Academy near the top of his class and was commissioned in the Marine Corps in 1935. He served in China with the 4th Marines and was assigned to various Marine barracks and the USS *Pennsylvania* until joining the 9th Marines in 1942. He served as a battalion commander for two years fighting on Bougainville, Guam, and Iwo Jima. His awards for valor included the Navy Cross. After the war he served in various school assignments and then on higher staffs as well as with the CIA. He took command of the 2d Marines in 1956, then served four years as Assistant to the Vice President for National Security Affairs (Richard Nixon). In 1961 he became the assistant commander of the 3d MarDiv, and then the commander. For the next two years he held various staff assignments at Headquarters, Marine Corps, then held the dual assignment of commanding Camp Pendleton and 4th MarDiv. He organized and commanded 5th MarDiv in 1967 and was then assigned as Deputy Commander, III MAF. He was promoted to lieutenant general in June 1967 and assumed command of III MAF, at the time the largest combined force ever led by a Marine. He commanded the force until March 1969 and then served as Deputy Director of the CIA until becoming the twenty-fifth Commandant of the Marine Corps in 1972. General Cushman retired in 1975 and died in 1985.

MajGen Rathvon McC. Tompkins (USMC) was Commanding General, 3d MarDiv. He was born in 1912 and commissioned into the Marine Corps in 1935. In his 36 years of service he won every medal for valor except the Medal of Honor. In World War II he fought on Guadalcanal, Tarawa, and Saipan with the 2d MarDiv. He commanded the 5th Marines in the 1st MarDiv in Korea. MajGen Tompkins arrived in Vietnam in November

The key commander on the ground at Khe Sanh was Col David E. Lownds, Commanding Officer, 26th Regimental Combat Team (Reinforced). He sports the handlebar mustache he wore throughout the battle as well as a 10lb 3oz M1955 armored vest or "flak jacket," worn virtually round the clock by all on the base.

1967 and assumed command of the 3d MarDiv, which he commanded until May 1968. He retired in 1971 and died in 1999.

Col David E. Lownds (USMC), Commanding Officer, 26th Marines, was born in 1920 in Massachusetts. Commissioned in the Marine Corps in 1942, he fought as a platoon commander in the 4th MarDiv on Roi-Namur, Saipan, and Iwo Jima. Wounded on several occasions, he left the Marines at the end of 1945. He was recalled as a reservist in 1950 for the Korean War and served in staff assignments in the 2d MarDiv. After the war he served in a variety of staff positions from battalion to Headquarters, Marine Corps, including operations, intelligence and executive officer, and as a reserve unit inspector-instructor. In 1958 he took command of 3/8 Marines. In 1964–65 he was the plans officer for 2d MarDiv and then the Marine force operations officer during the 1965 Dominican Republic intervention. He went to Vietnam in July 1967 to assume command of the 26th Marines on August 12, which he commanded throughout the defense of Khe Sanh until April 18, 1968, when Col Bruce F. Meyers relieved him. He was awarded the Navy Cross for his efforts. He soon retired and now resides in Florida.

Battalion-level commanders at Khe Sanh from January 20–April 1, 1968:

1st Battalion, 9th Marines	LtCol John F. Mitchell (to March 31)
	LtCol John J.H. Cahill
1st Battalion, 13th Marines [artillery]	LtCol John A. Hennelly
1st Battalion, 26th Marines	LtCol James B. Wilkinson (to February 29)
	LtCol Frederick J. McEwan
2d Battalion, 26th Marines	LtCol Francis J. Heath, Jr.
3d Battalion, 26th Marines	LtCol Harry L. Aderman (to March 14)
	LtCol John C. Studt
Forward Operations Base 3	Maj Lucius J. Campbell (to undetermined date February)
	Maj David C. Smith (to undetermined date March)
	LtCol Roy W. Bahr
37th Ranger Battalion	Capt Hoang Pho (ARVN)

NORTH VIETNAMESE COMMANDERS

The Route 9-Khe Sanh Front Command was established by the NVA in December 1967 to control the operation around KSCB. It was under the command of **MajGen Tran Quy Hai**, Assistant Chief of Staff, People's Army of Vietnam (PAVN) General Staff. He was one of the original Viet Minh officers, commanding infantry units during the war with France. Prior to becoming Assistant Chief of Staff, PAVN General Staff, he mainly held rear service and air-defense roles, experience that served him well during the Khe Sanh campaign. After the war he served in military justice assignments and retired in 1980.

The Front political commissar was **Le Quang Dao**, Deputy Director of the General Political Directorate, PAVN. He was a member of the Central Committee and was previously deeply involved with operations in Laos. After the war he was responsible for military youth organizations. **MajGen Tran Van Quang** was the commander of Tri-Thien Front with **MajGen Le Chuong** the political commissar.

Col Tran Tho, the Deputy Operational Commander, held a major responsibility for logistics. He retired as a major general responsible for

Two AN/TPQ-10 radars of Marine Airfield Traffic Control Unit 62 used to guide aircraft to their target. This radar emitted a beam that locked onto the aircraft. With data provided by the Fire Support Control Center the controller transmitted the targeting information with the enemy position, ordnance ballistics, wind speed and direction, and other necessary data. At a computer-calculated predetermined release point the controller directed the pilot when to release his load. In the foreground is a fire truck displaying minor fragmentation holes, its windshield and other windows removed because of fragmentation damage.

rear services. **Senior Col Nguyen Song Sy**, former Deputy Director of the General Rear Service Department, took command of Group 559 (a specialist supply formation) prior to the siege.

Nothing is known of the NVA division and lower echelon commanders. It can be assumed divisional and regimental commanders were experienced veterans of the war with France, tough, and dedicated to the cause. PAVN officers by necessity had to be ideologically motivated. They operated in a dual-command system down to company level with a political commissar part of the decision-making process. The system had its flaws, but because of the degree to which it was integrated into the armed forces and all aspects of North Vietnamese life, such an arrangement was essential in the view of North Vietnam's Communist Party. The strong mix of ideological integration, unorthodox military education and development, and the involvement in a lengthy and difficult war where self-sacrifice was an everyday occurrence, all shaped the nature of the NVA's officers. They were categorized as "careerists," those emphasizing military skill and familiarity with military technology, or "devotees," those devoted to and totally enmeshed in the Party's cause and placing hopes on complete loyalty to that cause.

OPPOSING FORCES

FREE WORLD FORCES

All US forces in the Republic of Vietnam were under US Military Assistance Command, Vietnam (MACV), led by Army general William C. Westmoreland. South Vietnam was divided into four areas, designated Corps Tactical Zones (CTZ) numbered I to IV from north to south. These corps zones had been organized by the ARVN, but US forces basically overlaid their command arrangements on them. I CTZ encompassed South Vietnam's five northernmost provinces and US forces in the zone were under the control of III Marine Amphibious Force (III MAF), a corps-level command that also controlled US Army units. Free World military forces in Vietnam were not under a combined integrated command; US and Vietnamese forces operated under their own commands, though they were closely coordinated and ARVN units were often placed under US control.

III MAF controlled the 1st and 3d MarDivs plus the Army's 1st Cavalry (Airmobile) and Americal Divisions, as well as brigades detached from the 4th Infantry and 82d Airborne Divisions. The 2d Korean Marine Brigade was also attached. Army units in I CTZ were administered and supported by a temporary command known at MACV Forward, established on February 9, 1968 as the NVA offensive continued. It became Provisional Corps, Vietnam, on March 10 and was assigned to the relief of Khe Sanh.

Two strings of bombs march from left to right delivered during a B-52D "Arc Light" strike. Dropped from 40,000ft, the bombers were en route back to Guam on their 2,800 mile 10–12-hour round trip by the time their bombs struck. Other B-52s flew from Thailand and Okinawa.

The 1st MarDiv (1st, 5th, 7th, 11th [artillery] Marines), "The Old Breed," was headquartered at Da Nang on the coast well south of Quang Tri province. The 3d MarDiv was headquartered at Hue on the coast halfway between the DMZ and Da Nang. In March, while the siege was under way, the headquarters moved to Quang Tri City.

The 3d MarDiv (3d, 4th, 9th, 12th [artillery] Marines), "The Fighting Third," had been organized in September 1942. It fought on Bougainville, Guam, and Iwo Jima and was deactivated at the end of 1945. It was reactivated in January 1952 and stationed in Japan. In 1956 it relocated to Okinawa where it remains to this day. It served in Vietnam from May 1965 to November 1969 and was responsible for operations at Khe Sanh.

The primary Marine unit at Khe Sanh was the 26th Marines, "The Professionals," actually a regiment assigned to the recently reactivated 5th MarDiv in California, but attached to the 3d MarDiv since April 1967. With the California-based 1st MarDiv and Okinawa-based 3d MarDiv both in Vietnam, the 5th MarDiv (13th [artillery], 26th, 27th, 28th Marines), "Spearhead Division," was reactivated in March 1966 to serve as a Pacific contingency force. Nevertheless, two of its regiments would fight in Vietnam. The 5th MarDiv had originally been activated in January 1944, fought on Iwo Jima, its only combat operation, performed occupation duty in Japan, and was deactivated in February 1946.

The 26th Marines had originally been activated in January 1944. After fighting on Iwo Jima it was detached from the 5th MarDiv and assigned to occupation duty in Japan, followed by the Palau Islands, and was deactivated in March 1946. It was reactivated in March 1966 at Camp Pendleton, California, and the 1st and 2d Battalions deployed to Vietnam in August 1966, attached to the 3d MarDiv. The 3d Battalion arrived in November and the regimental headquarters, which had been on Okinawa since August, deployed to Phu Bai in April 1967, leaving a rear detachment on Okinawa. Designated 26th Regimental Landing Team (Forward), the unit conducted several operations in northern I CTZ through 1967. 1st Battalion garrisoned KSCB in May 1967, relieving the 3d Marines after the Hill Battles. The 3d Battalion arrived at Khe Sanh in

June and the 2d Battalion in January 1968. The 26th RLT was the primary unit occupying KSCB and the northern hill positions during the siege.

Another participant in the battle was 1st Battalion, 9th Marines, known as "The Walking Dead" due to their lengthy service in Vietnam. The 9th was one of the Corps' older regiments having first served from 1917–19. It was reactivated in February 1942 and assigned to the 3d MarDiv until deactivated in December 1945. The "Striking Ninth" was briefly reactivated from 1947–49. When reactivated again in March 1952 it was assigned to the 3d MarDiv and the 1st Battalion arrived in Vietnam in June 1965.

The 3d Marines was the major player in the Hill Battles, augmented by elements of the 9th and 26th Marines. The 3d Marines had originally served from 1916–22. It was reactivated once more in June 1942 to operate alongside the 9th Marines with the 3d MarDiv, and deactivated in January 1946. Reactivated in 1947, it was again deactivated in 1949. It was reactivated in June 1951 because of the Korean War, assigned to the 3d Marine Brigade and then the 3d MarDiv, with which it has served ever since. Arriving in Vietnam in April 1965, it was the first Marine regiment deployed there.

In 1968 a Marine infantry regiment[13] had a 222-man regimental headquarters company with a regimental headquarters, company headquarters, scout-sniper platoon, and communication platoon. The three 1,649-man infantry battalions each had four 216-man rifle companies and a 385-man headquarters and service company. The H&S company was organized into a battalion headquarters, company headquarters, and communication, service, antitank (8 x 106mm M40A1 recoilless rifles), and mortar (8 x 81mm M29 mortars) platoons plus a flamethrower section (8 x M7-2 flamethrowers), the latter seldom manned in Vietnam.

A rifle company had a nine-man headquarters and a 66-man weapons platoon with machine gun (6 x 7.62mm M60 machine guns), antitank (6 x 3.5in M20A1B1 bazookas), and mortar (3 x 60mm M19 mortars) sections. Its three 47-man rifle platoons had a five-man headquarters and three 14-man rifle squads armed with M16 rifles and a single 40mm M79 grenade launcher.

A regimental landing team was habitually task-organized with a number of supporting units attached, and the 26th RLT was no exception. It was heavily augmented by additional units not normally attached to support the regiment and the base. Appended combat units included 1st Battalion, 13th Marines with its three 105mm batteries and a battery of 4.2in mortars augmented by 1st Provisional 155mm Howitzer Battery. All batteries had six artillery pieces and all were deployed in KSCB itself, with the exception of three Battery C 105mm weapons located on Hill 881S and two 4.2in mortars on Hill 861. The Marines in the base and surrounding outposts had at least 32 x 81mm and 48 x 60mm mortars at their disposal, plus a few of each in FOB-3 (which also had a 4.2in mortar). The 37th Rangers had four 60mm, one 81mm, and one 106mm rifle. There were six 90mm gun-armed

Artillery and Mortars at Khe Sanh	
Weapon	**Range meters (feet)**
United States	
60mm M19 mortar	2,000 (6,500)
81mm M29 mortar	3,650 (11,500)
4.2in M30 mortar	5,500 (18,000)
105mm M101A1 howitzer	11,000 (36,000)
155mm M114A1 howitzer	12,950 (42,500)
175mm M107 self-propelled gun	32,700 (107,000)
NVA	
60mm Type 31 and 63 mortars	1,530 (5,000)
82mm BM37 mortar	3,000 (9,800)
120mm HM43 mortar	5,700 (18,700)
122mm D74 gun	24,000 (79,000)
130mm M46 gun	27,500 (90,000)
152mm D20 gun-howitzer	17,265 (57,000)
107mm Type 63 12-tube rocket launcher	8,500 (28,000)
122mm DKB 1-tube rocket launcher	10,000 (33,000)

Mortar notes: *The NVA used some captured US 81mm M1 and M29 mortars as well as 60mm M19 mortars, while the Marines used a few captured 82mm BM37 mortars with US ammunition.*

The angular dotted white lines are "Arc Light" bomb swathes crisscrossing around Khe Sanh. Hills 881N and 881S are indicated, as is KSCB, the base encircled in black below and to the right of the label.

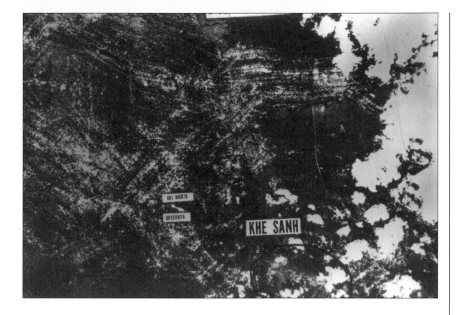

M48A3 Patton tanks, three each from 2d and 3d Platoons, Company B, 3d Tank Battalion. Company A (-), 3d Antitank Battalion (soon redesignated Antitank Company, 3d Tank Battalion) had two platoons, each with five M50A1 Ontos antitank vehicles each armed with six 106mm recoilless rifles. There was, in addition, an array of small reconnaissance, communication, engineer, motor transport, shore party (essentially stevedores), medical (manned by Navy personnel), logistical, and service detachments.

Four Navy Mobile Construction Battalion (Seabee) detachments provided most of the engineer support. Army units included signal, smoke, and AN/MPQ-4 countermortar radar detachments, plus a composite automatic weapons platoon with two M42A1 "Duster" self-propelled dual 40mm antiaircraft guns and two 2½ ton M35A2 truck-mounted quad .50-cal M55 machine guns. Additional fire support was provided by Army 175mm self-propelled guns of Battery A, 8th Battalion, 4th Artillery, and Batteries B and C, 2d Battalion, 94th Artillery, at Camp Carroll, and Battery A, 2d Battalion, at the Rockpile.

FOB-3 was the most northwestern base employed by MACV-Studies and Observation Group's (MACV-SOG), Command and Control North (CCN). This highly classified operation conducted reconnaissance and small-scale strike operations inside Laos, North Vietnam, and South Vietnam, mainly targeting the Ho Chi Minh Trail. While largely manned by US Special Forces (USSF), SOG was not a component of the in-country 5th Special Forces Group, but a joint unconventional warfare task force directly under MACV control. FOB strength varied during the siege, but included 131 USSF and other Americans and 457 indigenous Special Commando Unit personnel – Chinese Nungs, Cambodians, Montagnards, and Vietnamese. Besides staff and support personnel, FOB had a large number of reconnaissance teams (two USSF, six indigenous personnel), a few Spike Teams (three USSF, nine indigenous) for reinforcing and aiding in the extraction of recon teams, and a Hatchet Team (six USSF, 32 indigenous) to hit targets of opportunity discovered by the recon teams. FOB units also performed bomb-damage assessment and conducted communications intercept operations. FOB-3 was augmented by rotating 1st Special Forces Group 12-man A-teams from Okinawa.

FOB-3 was on the south side of the base and actually just outside it, linking the Red and Gray Sectors. Originally an FOB-1 launch site had been established at Khe Sanh village in 1966, but it moved into the moated Old French Fort in the summer of 1967 and became FOB-3 in September. Immediately before the siege, FOB-3 began to build a new and very well-protected compound, completed in mid February 1968, on the south side of base. Its facilities were comparatively comfortable and boasted amenities only dreamed of by the Marines. It included a large helicopter LZ to launch and recover its teams. Reconnaissance operations were reduced during the siege, but still continued into Laos. Special helicopters would arrive to pick up recon teams and insert them across the border. The Marines distrusted the indigenous commandos and were suspicious of the Green Berets, accusing them of "being a law unto themselves." No indigenous personnel could enter KSCB at any time, and American FOB personnel could only enter the base in daylight. In addition, the Marines placed wire barriers, mines, and fighting bunkers on the perimeter behind the FOB, fearing the indigenous commandos would switch sides.

Another element placed in FOB-3 included Marines, Company O, 3d Combined Action Group along with Huong Hoa District Headquarters evacuated from Khe Sanh village. Company O's three CAP platoons consisted of about a dozen Marines and a similar number of Montagnard Popular Force troops.[14]

The 37th ARVN Ranger Battalion (Tieu-Doàn 37 Biêt Dông Quân) arrived on January 27 and was deployed around the east and southeast ends of the base outside Gray Sector. Again the Marines maintained defensive positions behind the Rangers due to a basic lack of faith in the ARVN soldiers. It appears that the NVA also thought the Rangers might be suspect as they deployed a reinforced NVA battalion in front of them and the only actual NVA assaults on the base struck the Rangers' positions. In their defense the ARVN Rangers repulsed every attack with ease. Other than the four US advisors, water and supply details, and wounded men, ARVN Rangers were not allowed to enter Marine lines. The 37th had seen a great deal of action throughout I CTZ since its formation in 1964 and was far below its authorized strength of 646. The battalion had a headquarters company (headquarters, reconnaissance, and heavy weapons platoons, the latter with a 106mm recoilless rifle, an 81mm mortar, and two M60 machine guns) and four 80–90-man rifle companies, each with three 20–25-man platoons with an M60, plus a weapons section with a 60mm mortar and an additional M60.

Overall strength at Khe Sanh fluctuated with casualties and replacements while FOB-3 and the 37th Ranger Battalion were often not included in the totals. The various supporting detachments numbered

A Marine battalion had eight 106mm M40A1 recoilless rifle mounted on M274A1 "Mechanical Mule" 1/2 ton weapons carriers. Fitted atop the 106mm is a .50-cal M8C spotting rifle, using different ammunition than the .50-cal machine gun. It allowed the gunner to accurately adjust his aim before firing the main gun. The "One-Oh-Six" was used for supporting and suppressive fire, countermortar, and countersniping.

only a few hundred additional men. The Marine battalions were 300–400 men below strength. The strength of the major units at Khe Sanh in late January is detailed below:

HQ Company, 26th Marines (Forward)	191[15]
1st Battalion, 26th Marines	1,301
2d Battalion, 26th Marines	1,254
3d Battalion, 26th Marines	1,279
1st Battalion, 9th Marines	1,192
1st Battalion, 13th Marines [artillery]	397
Forward Operations Base 3	588
37th Ranger Battalion	318[16]

The 1st CavDiv (Airmobile) under MajGen John J. Tolson III would play a prominent role in the relief of Khe Sanh, Operation *Pegasus*. It was essentially a light infantry division with three organic aviation battalions and three companies, providing it with unprecedented battlefield mobility and aerial firepower. Almost 350 UH-1 Huey, C-47 Chinook, OH-6 Cayuse, and UH-1 attack helicopters allowed it to lift one third of its infantry battalions at a time. Its nine infantry battalions bore traditional cavalry designations, 1st Battalion (Airmobile), 7th Cavalry, for example.

NORTH VIETNAMESE ARMY

The People's Army of Vietnam (PAVN), or NVA, was a conventionally organized and equipped army under professional, but highly politicized, leadership. The PAVN was organized from the Viet Minh in 1954 after a successful war with France and they were by no means "guerrillas."

Administratively the northern portion of South Vietnam from the Central Highlands to the DMZ was known to the NVA as Military Region 5. In 1966 the NVA further subdivided the area establishing the Tri-Thien Military Region B4 ("B" was the code designation for commands in South Vietnam) to control operations in South Vietnam's two important northernmost provinces, Quang Tri and Thua Thien. At the end of 1967 the forces assigned to this front included those on both sides of the DMZ:

304 Division	675 Artillery Regiment
320 Division	208 Antiaircraft Artillery Regiment
324B Division	214 Antiaircraft Artillery Regiment
325C Division	228 Antiaircraft Artillery Regiment
270 Independent Regiment	7 Engineer Regiment
16 Artillery Regiment	198 Tank Battalion
45 Artillery Regiment	independent engineer battalion
84 Artillery Regiment	independent signal battalion
204 Artillery Regiment	

In preparation for the Khe Sanh operation, on December 6, 1967 the Central Military Party Committee established the Route 9-Khe Sanh Party Committee and the Route 9-Khe Sanh Front Military Command, codenamed B5-T8. Its headquarters were located at Sap Lit in Laos west of the North/South Vietnam border. Group 559 (*Doan 559*) had been established in 1959, when construction of the Ho Chi Minh Trail was

Fifteen 105mm M101A1 howitzers were positioned on KSCB and three on 881S. Battery B, 1st Battalion, 13th Marines actually had a refurbished 105mm that the battery had used in World War II when the howitzer was known as the M2A1. Flat tires caused by fragmentation were a constant problem for crews as the unleveled gun's accuracy would be affected and uneven recoil would throw off the aim for subsequent rounds.

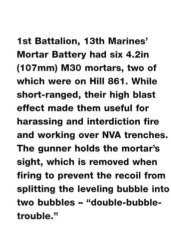

1st Battalion, 13th Marines' Mortar Battery had six 4.2in (107mm) M30 mortars, two of which were on Hill 861. While short-ranged, their high blast effect made them useful for harassing and interdiction fire and working over NVA trenches. The gunner holds the mortar's sight, which is removed when firing to prevent the recoil from splitting the leveling bubble into two bubbles – "double-bubble-trouble."

begun to funnel units and supplies to the south through Laos and Cambodia. This strategic rear-services organization was assigned transport, engineer, antiaircraft, and communication units with over 25,000 troops. It was instrumental in sustaining the Khe Sanh front.

The primary divisions assigned to the front were 304 and 325C Divisions. The 320 and 324B Divisions would support the operation; 304 and 320 Divisions were among the original six NVA divisions (304, 308, 312, 316, 320, and 325). The letters "B," "C," and "D" tagged onto unit designations indicated "cloned" divisions formed by the original unlettered division. This system is very confusing to order-of-battle specialists, particularly as even North Vietnamese writings sometimes omitted the letters. The 325C Division, for example, is the third division, bearing the same number as its parent 325 Division. The component regiments and other units would bear the same letter indicator. Wartime intelligence often omitted the letter from component regiments. Some sources indicate 325C as "325" and many more list 324B as "324." It has never been ascertained for certain which is actually correct.

A full-strength NVA infantry division (*su doan bo binh*) had 9,600 troops organized into three infantry regiments, an artillery regiment (or battalion in some instances), antiaircraft, engineer, signal, and medical battalions, and a transport company. The artillery regiments were mostly armed with 82mm and 120mm mortars. Certain units stationed in North Vietnam were equipped with some conventional light artillery, but more portable weapons were substituted when they deployed to South Vietnam.

Infantry regiments included about 2,500 troops with three 600-man battalions. Most units were typically understrength, with battalions deployed to Khe Sanh numbering 400–500 men. Regardless of organization tables, NVA units' armament varied considerably as a result of long campaigning, the availability of weapons, and how they configured for specific operations. Regiments typically had a recoilless rifle company (8–12 Soviet 73mm SPG-9 or Chinese 75mm Type 52 recoilless rifles and US 57mm M18A1 or Chinese Type 36 recoilless rifles), a mortar company with 6–8 82mm mortars, an antiaircraft company with 6–10 12.7mm DShKM38/46 machine guns, plus small engineer, transport, signal, and medical companies. Rifle companies were organized into one weapons and three rifle platoons. The latter included three squads, each with a 7.62mm RPD light machine gun, an RPG-2 or -7 (B40, B41) antitank weapon, 7.62mm AK-47 assault rifles,

The 1st Provisional 155mm Howitzer Battery was part of 1/13 Marines and provided counterbattery fire. Six M114A1 medium howitzers were assigned to the battery. Concrete firing platforms were poured for the 105mm and 155mm howitzers to provide a stable platform for more accurate shooting.

Army 175mm M107 self-propelled guns firing from the Rockpile and Camp Carroll provided counterbattery fire for Khe Sanh. This one belongs to Battery A, 2d Battalion, 94th Artillery. While the longest ranged gun in the Army's inventory, it was not the most accurate, being an area fire weapon.

and possibly a captured M79 grenade launcher. The weapons platoon would have a few 7.62mm SGM machine guns, 2–4 60mm Chinese Type 31 or 63 mortars, and sometimes a couple of 57mm recoilless rifles. There simply was no standard allocation. The fighting around Khe Sanh would see some of the first combat use of the RPG-7.

Little is known of the NVA artillery units at Khe Sanh. Units mentioned include 68, 164 and 675 Artillery Regiments, and 4 Battalion, 84, 368B, and Van An Rocket Artillery Regiments plus 24 Artillery Battalion. The confusion exists because deployed NVA units were identified by code designations and names and they were frequently changed during an operation. The artillery was under a central command, sometimes identified as 559 Artillery Group. US intelligence was unable to determine the numbers and types of artillery units or the number of weapons used at Khe Sanh, although one source mentions up to 200 guns and heavy mortars, which seems an overestimation. One National Security assessment given to the White House was nothing more than a duplication of the numbers and calibers of artillery the Viet

The NVA infantryman was a skilled, determined, and tenacious opponent. Typically uniformed in green fatigues with a fiber pith helmet, he was lightly armed and equipped. The soldier in the foreground is armed with a 40mm (over-caliber warhead diameter is 85mm) RPG-2 (B40) rocket-propelled grenade; the RPG-7 (B41) was a much improved version. It was a marginal antipersonnel weapon, but was effective against bunkers and light armored vehicles.

Minh employed at Dien Bien Phu. Considering the number of rounds fired on Khe Sanh there may not have been a great deal of artillery present, possibly only six to nine batteries at the most, plus rocket units.

Five NVA divisions were involved to varying degrees around Khe Sanh. The main assault divisions were 304 and 325C with 320 supporting, 324B in reserve, and 308 "Vanguard" later involved in resisting Operation *Pegasus*. The 304 and 320 were among the four "Steel and Iron" divisions (312 and 316 being the others) that could be committed to the south only by the PAVN General Staff. The reality is that the NVA order of battle is simply not fully known; we cannot be sure which regiments from which divisions were present. To cloud the issue, Divisions were not consistent in the designations with which they referred to their constituent regiments. Unsurprisingly, intelligence summaries and post-operation studies by different organizations and agencies are in conflict. Assessments of 325C Division range from all three regiments present to just one (18). It is surmised that other divisions sent complete battalions or replacement drafts.

Other units identified included 203 Tank Regiment with two battalions, 7 Engineer Regiment, and sapper (reconnaissance/commando) companies. Identified antiaircraft units included 74 and 75 Battalions armed with 12.7mm DShKM38/46 and 37mm M1939 weapons. The 367, 368, and 377 Air Defense Divisions north of the DMZ may also have deployed elements to the Khe Sanh area.

ORDERS OF BATTLE

Khe Sanh

US Order of Battle

Hill Fights, 24 April–13 May 1967

3d Marines (-)(+)	24 Apr–13 May
HQ Company, 3d Marines	24 Apr–13 May
2d Battalion, 3d Marines (+)	24 Apr–13 May
H&S Company (-)(+)	
Company E (+)	
Company F (+)	
Company G (+)	
Company H (+)	
Company A, 1st Battalion, 26th Marines	11–13 May
Company B, 1st Battalion, 26th Marines	11–13 May
Company C, 1st Battalion, 26th Marines	13 May
Company D, 1st Battalion, 26th Marines	11–13 May
Company E, 2d Battalion, 26th Marines	12–13 May
3d Platoon, Company B, 1st Amphibian Tractor Battalion	24 Apr–13 May
2d Platoon, Company A, 3d Antitank Battalion	24 Apr–13 May
3d Platoon, Company B, 3d Reconnaissance Battalion	24 Apr–13 May
3d Battalion, 3d Marines (-)(+)	25 Apr–13 May
Command Group	25 Apr–13 May
Company K	25–27 Apr
Company M	27 Apr–1 May
Company D, 1st Battalion, 9th Marines	25–27 Apr
Company K, 3d Battalion, 9th Marines	25 Apr–13 May
Company M, 3d Battalion, 9th Marines	29 Apr–13 May
Company F, 2d Battalion, 3d Marines	1–3 May
Company C, 1st Battalion, 26th Marines	5–13 May
Company A, 1st Battalion, 26th Marines	12–13 May
Base Defense/Reserve	

Company B, 1st Battalion, 9th Marines	24–27 Apr
Company F, 2d Battalion, 3d Marines	27 Apr–1 May
Company E, 2d Battalion, 9th Marines	1–12 May
Company C, 1st Battalion, 9th Marines	4–5 May
1st Battalion, 26th Marines	12–13 May
Direct Support Artillery	
Battery F (+), 2d Battalion, 12th Marines	24 Apr–13 May
Battery B, 1st Battalion, 12th Marines	27 Apr–11 May
Battery A, 1st Battalion, 12th Marines	13 May

Siege of Khe Sanh, 20 January–1 April 1968

All units present 20 January to 1 April unless shown otherwise.

26th Marines (-)(+) (Regimental Landing Team 26 (Forward))	
HQ Company (-)	
1st Battalion, 26th Marines	
2d Battalion, 26th Marines	
3d Battalion, 26th Marines	
1st Battalion, 9th Marines	22 Jan
1st Battalion, 13th Marines (artillery)	
1st Provisional 155mm Howitzer Battery	
Antitank Company (-), 3d Tank Battalion	
Company O, 3d Combined Action Group	
Company A, 3d Shore Party Battalion	24 Jan
3d Clearing Platoon, Company C, 3d Medical Battalion	24 Jan
3d Platoon, Company D, 3d Reconnaissance Battalion	
1st Platoon, Company A, 5th Reconnaissance Battalion	
Otter Platoon, H&S Company, 3d Motor Transport Battalion	
Detachment, Company B, 3d Tank Battalion	
Detachment, 1st Searchlight Battery	
Detachment, 3d Engineer Battalion	
Detachment, H&S Company, 3d Shore Party Battalion	24 Jan
Detachment, Company A, 9th Motor Transport Battalion	
Detachment, Company B, 9th Motor Transport Battalion	
Detachment, Sub-Unit No.1, 1st Radio Battalion	
Detachment, 3d Dental Company	
Detachment, HQ Company, HQ Battalion, 3d Mar Div	
(postal exchange, photo, air observers, staff augmentation, etc)	
Detachment, Communication Company, HQ Battalion, 3d Mar Div	
Detachment, 5th Communication Battalion	
Detachment, 7th Communication Battalion	
Logistics Support Unit, Force Logistics Command	
Sub-Team No.1, 17th Interrogator-Translator Team	
Detachment 01, HQ and Maintenance Squadron, MAG 16	
Detachment 01, Marine Observation Squadron 6, MAG 16	15 Mar
Detachment 2*, Air Support Squadron 3, Marine Air Control Group	18–16 Jan
Detachment, HQ and Maintenance Squadron 36, MAG 36	
Detachment, Marine Air Traffic Control Unit 62, MAG 36	

* *Air Support Radar Team Bravo*

US Navy	
Detachment, Naval Mobile Construction Battalion 5	
Detachment, Naval Mobile Construction Battalion 10	20 Jan–19 Feb
Detachment, Naval Mobile Construction Battalion 53	
Detachment Bravo, Naval Mobile Construction Battalion Unit 301	
US Army	
Forward Operations Base 3, Command & Control North, MACV-SOG	
Detachment A-101 (+), Company C, 5th Special Forces Group (Airborne) †	
Lang Vei CIDG Camp Strike Force †	
101st–104th Camp Strike Force Companies †	
12th Company, Pleiku Mobile Strike Force †	
1st–3d Combat Reconnaissance Platoons †	

† *Ceased to exist 7 February*

Section, Battery A, 1st Battalion (Automatic Weapons, Self-Propelled), 44th Artillery‡	
Section, Battery G (.50-cal Machine Gun), 65th Artillery‡	
Detachment, 238th Artillery Detachment (Countermortar Radar)	22 Jan
Detachment, 1st Platoon, 25th Chemical Company (Smoke)	9 Feb
544th Signal Detachment (Tactical Communications)	
Mobile Advisory Team 4 (Huong Hoa District)	

Battalion Advisory Team (37th Ranger Battalion)   27 Jan
‡ *Operated as a composite platoon*

US Air Force
    Operating Location AJ, 15th Aerial Port Squadron
    Detachment, 366th Transport Squadron, 366th Combat Support Group
    Detachment, 903d Aeromedical Evacuation Squadron
    Detachment A, 834th Air Division

ARVN
    37th Ranger Battalion   27 Jan
        84th Company, 8th Airborne Battalion   6 Apr
    Huong Hoa District HQ
        915th Regional Force Company   20–23 Jan

Operation *Pegasus*, 1–15 April 1968

1st Cavalry Division (Airmobile)
    1st Squadron (Air), 9th Cavalry   25 Mar
    1st Brigade, 1st Cavalry Division (Airmobile)   5 Apr
        1st Battalion (Airmobile), 8th Cavalry
        2d Battalion (Airmobile), 8th Cavalry
        1st Battalion (Airmobile), 12th Cavalry
    2d Brigade, 1st Cavalry Division (Airmobile)   3 Apr
        1st Battalion (Airmobile), 5th Cavalry
        2d Battalion (Airmobile), 5th Cavalry
        2d Battalion (Airmobile), 12th Cavalry
    3d Brigade, 1st Cavalry Division (Airmobile)   1 Apr
        1st Battalion (Airmobile), 7th Cavalry
        2d Battalion (Airmobile), 7th Cavalry
        5th Battalion (Airmobile), 7th Cavalry
    1st Marines, 1st Marine Division   1 Apr
        1st Battalion, 1st Marines
        2d Battalion, 1st Marines
        2d Battalion, 3d Marines
        3d Airborne Task Force, ARVN Airborne Division   7 Apr
        3d Airborne Battalion
        6th Airborne Battalion
        8th Airborne Battalion
    26th Marines (+) at KSCB under operational control

---

13 A Marine infantry regiment was designated with an identifying number only thus, 26th Marines; "infantry" and "regiment" were not part of its official designation. In Vietnam the 1st, 3d, 4th, 5th, 7th, 9th, 26th and 27th Marines were infantry and the 11th, 12th and 13th were artillery. Marine battalions and even companies could be attached to different regiments and battalions as necessary.
14 Collectively called "Ruff/Puffs," the Regional Forces were provincial security forces while the Popular Forces were village self-defense militia.
15 The rear detachment on Okinawa numbered 275.
16 Colonel Pho Hoang asserts he had "no less than 400 men" and that replacements for casualties were provided from Da Nang.
17 Detached to Hue.
18 Maintained supply route west of Khe Sanh.
19 Detached to eastern Quang Tri.
20 Remained in North Vietnam.
21 Attached.

THE SIEGE

ISOLATION OF KHE SANH AND OPENING MOVES

The end of December 1967 found KSCB manned by a 26th Marines rump headquarters, its 1st and 3d Battalions, a composite artillery battery, and minimal supporting elements. Six Marine tanks and ten Ontos antitank vehicles plus a pair each of Army quad .50-cal and twin 40mm Duster guns had all been there since July. In the same month, the Marines dispatched a convoy of 85 trucks and two 175mm guns to Khe Sanh. The NVA ambushed the convoy on QL9 west of Camp Carroll. Rather than endanger the big guns, they and their support were returned to Camp Carroll while the convoy continued on to Khe Sanh. The NVA cut QL9 in August, but the last US convoy making it through was in July. The actual reason for sending the 175mm guns to Khe Sanh is unknown. They would have been useless for base defense as their minimum indirect fire range was 7,200m. They would have been useful for counterbattery fire on Co Roc, but this was unforeseen at the time. It is speculated that they were intended to support MACV-SOG missions inside Laos and interdict segments of the Ho Chi Minh Trail.

With the discovery of increasing NVA activity in the area on December 21, plans were made to reinforce the base and planning for air support, Operation *Niagara*, began on January 5. The next day Westmoreland advised Cushman of III MAF, "The anticipated build-up of enemy forces in the western DMZ area provides an opportunity to plan a comprehensive intelligence collection effort and to make coordination of B-52 and tactical air strikes. We should be prepared to surprise and disrupt enemy plans for an offensive against Khe Sanh with heavy bombing attacks on a sustained basis." Seventh Air Force initiated a comprehensive intelligence collection effort and dedicated B-52s to support Khe Sanh, their first use in a tactical support role.

President Lyndon B. Johnson became almost obsessive about Khe Sanh. He was briefed daily and pored over maps and a terrain board, telling General Earl Wheeler, Chairman of the Joint Chiefs of Staff, "I don't want any damn Dinbinphoo."

Within two weeks it was determined that two NVA divisions were converging on Khe Sanh. Patrols around the base

The M50A1 Ontos (Greek for "The Thing"), commonly known to marines as the "Pig," mounted six 106mm M40A1C recoilless rifles, four with spotting rifles, and a .30-cal M1919A4 machine gun. The 8½ton antitank vehicle had a crew of three. Counting six rounds in the tubes, only 18 rounds were carried. The rifles could be fired singly or volleyed at once. Firing high-explosive and flechette rounds the ten Ontos on KSCB would have been deadly to a massed infantry attack and were effectively used for suppressive and harassing fire.

continued to make contact. NVA sappers had cut gaps through the wire in places and re-closed them for future use. Col Lownds stated on January 10 that he expected an attack within ten days. On the 14th an eight-man patrol on the side of 881N was ambushed, losing two men. The remainder of the patrol was driven off, but the bodies were later recovered. Activity was steadily increasing. The next day 2/26 deployed from Phu Bai to Dong Ha for a new mission. Upon arrival it was notified to deploy immediately to Khe Sanh. 3d MarDiv felt Khe Sanh needed prompt reinforcement. The battalion arrived on January 16/17 and for the first time the entire 26th Marines were together since arriving in Vietnam. F/2/26 moved to and occupied Hill 558, finding it free of enemy. Most of the battalion moved in on the 17th. This position, with a large sprawling perimeter almost half the size of KSCB itself, blocked the Rao Qung gorge and a dirt road approaching KSCB from the northwest.

The hills were now defended by, from west to east (troop strengths are approximate):

881S	I/3/26 plus two platoons and M/3/26 Command Group (400)
861	K/3/26 plus two platoons A/1/26 (300)
861A	E/2/26 (200) – occupied February 5
558	2/26 - E/2/26 (1,000)
950	2d Platoon A/1/26 (50)

On January 15 Operation *Niagara* officially commenced to provide massive air support to KSCB. Before first light on the 20th, I/3/26 departed 881S to probe 881N to ascertain if the enemy occupied it in strength. The company moved up parallel ridge fingers in two columns 500 yards apart. Partway up 881N both columns were engaged by dug-in NVA. The company maneuvered to extract a pinned platoon and a helicopter was downed attempting to evacuate wounded. Though separated and taking casualties, the company fought its way to the crest, receiving artillery support from KSCB and mortar and recoilless rifle fire from the defenders on 881S. The 3d Platoon leader, 2dLt Thomas D. Brindly, "was everywhere … moved from flank to flank slapping his men on the back and urging them on." It was largely his leadership that carried the assault troops to the crest; he was the first man to reach the top, but he was downed by a sniper and posthumously awarded the Navy

Two 2½ ton M35A2 truck-mounted quad .50-cal M55 machine guns were contributed by the Army. The combined rate of fire of the four M2 machine guns was 2,000–2,600 rounds per minute with a 1,825m maximum effective range. Normally only the two upper or two lower pairs of guns were fired at once.

Cross. The 3/26 Command Group helicoptered to 881S and requested reinforcement from KSCB to clear 881N, but Col Lownds denied the request and ordered I/3/26 to break contact. He feared becoming engaged in a prolonged fight while expecting an NVA attack to unfold that night – I/3/26 withdrew with seven KIA and 35 WIA.

A/1/26 had accepted the surrender of an NVA lieutenant outside the base's perimeter that same afternoon. He was the commander of 95C Regiment's antiaircraft company and freely provided detailed information that 861 would be attacked in force that night. KSCB and the outposts were placed on Red Alert and higher headquarters notified.

On KSCB itself, L/3/26 and elements of I/3/26 defended the east end of the perimeter, the Red Sector. C/1/26 and elements of A/1/26 were on the north perimeter, Blue Sector. B/1/26 defended the east end and the south side, Gray Sector. D/1/26 was in reserve in the Ponderosa area near the base's center. FOB-3 was on the south-central side along with Company O, 3d Combined Action Group. The latter's 3d Platoon was 200m south of the FOB on the edge of Ta Con village, later to be pulled inside. Several helicopters were rotated to the base and remained in revetments for immediate reinforcement, resupply, and medical evacuation support for the outposts.

The base defenses were far from ready. Recently arrived units were not fully dug in and some key facilities were not yet underground. Much of the masses of ammunition rushed to the base to build a 30-day stock were not yet under cover. Another five days' stock was to be delivered soon.

The defecting NVA lieutenant revealed that 5 Battalion, 95C Regiment was to secure Hill 1015 and neutralize the Marine outpost on nearby 950. The regiment's 6 Battalion would attack 861 while 4 Battalion would attack the west end of the base's perimeter. At the same time, 101C Regiment reinforced by 8 Battalion, 29C Regiment, would attack the east end.

On the evening of the 20th a small reconnaissance patrol on Hill 869, 3km to the southwest of KSCB, reported it was surrounded. Artillery barrages ringed the patrol, keeping the NVA at bay, and it was later able to withdraw. At the same time events to the northwest on 861 began to unfold.

Soon after midnight some 300 NVA assaulted K/3/26 on the northwest side of 861 from close, concealed positions. The mortar-supported assault was launched so swiftly and at such close range that the Marines could not use artillery fire. Much of the company position was overrun and the commander wounded three times. The 3/26 Command Group was still on 881S since afternoon fog had grounded helicopters and they coordinated the defense operation. The Marines launched counterattacks and hand-to-hand combat was frequent. To keep their spirits up ammunition handlers bellowed the Marine Corps Hymn as they passed rounds to mortarmen. The mortars became so hot the crews used their water, then fruit juice to cool them, then urinated on the tubes. Sgt Mykle E. Stahl conducted a one-man counterattack to distract the NVA holding former Marine bunkers, allowing others to recover casualties. He killed two of three NVA attempting to capture him, knocked out three bunkers, and was found wounded three times still manning a .50-cal machine gun when his platoon reoccupied its position. For this action he received the Navy Cross. The NVA was forced to withdraw at 0530 hours while requesting reinforcements, which never appeared. Even though the combat was fierce and close, K/3/26 suffered only four KIA and 11 WIA, while 47 NVA dead were found and three wounded prisoners taken. It was found from the prisoners that they belonged to 4 Battalion, 95C Regiment rather than 6 Battalion as was reported by the defecting lieutenant. The other concerted attacks forecast for 950 and the base itself did not materialize, probably because of the failure to take 861.

To the east that same night attacks commenced to ensure QL9 remained cut. The 29C Regiment, 325C Division assaulted Hill 832, a remote outpost, and 48 and 66 Regiments, 320 Division, and 270 Independent Regiment's 47 Battalion cut QL9 and probed the district headquarters at Cam Lo. On the 23rd, 24 Regiment, 304 Division overran an ARVN outpost at Huoi Sun. Preparation time for these missions had been too short for the units tasked them, but nonetheless they were carried out.

As the NVA withdrew from Hill 861 at 0530 hours a barrage of artillery, mortars, and rockets struck KSCB without warning. Almost immediately Ammunition Supply Point No. 1 (ASP 1) near the east end detonated in a thunderous explosion of 1,100 tons of artillery, mortar, and recoilless rifle ammunition. Fragments, debris, and undetonated projectiles showered over the base. Eight Marines were killed in the blast and ammunition continued to "cook off" for two days. John Corbett in *West Dickens Avenue* recalls, "The horrendous noise hurts our eardrums so badly that in desperation we tear filters off cigarettes and plug them in our ears." Burning tear gas rolled over the base from ASP 1. Many Marines did not have gas masks and used wet towels. Marines carried smoldering projectiles by hand from around artillery positions. The generator for the fire-direction computer was knocked out, but firing data was calculated manually and counterbattery fired. Ammunition pallets continued to detonate through the day including a large stock of plastic explosives – this detonation was so large that it collapsed the roof of the 26th Marines COC 200m away. Newcomers were told a "300mm gun" caused the huge crater. NVA artillery tore up the airfield and its night-lighting system with 1,800ft

The twin 40mm M42A1 Duster self-propelled antiaircraft vehicle also mounted a 7.62mm M60 machine gun for close-in defense. The twin Bofors guns pumped out 240 rounds per minute of high-explosive tracer and armor-piercing tracer, the latter able to defeat a PT-76 tank. The Army provided two of these deadly weapons for Khe Sanh.

of runway remaining usable. One parked helicopter was destroyed and five damaged along with one destroyed on 881S.

Hampered by weather, C-123 transports began delivering replacement ammunition that night: 26 tons of it. By the 23rd the runway was cleared of debris, permitting its use by C-130s. Much of the engineer equipment, power generators, post exchange, and telephone lines were destroyed or damaged, but ammunition debris was cleared, damage repaired, and the wounded treated. The day's barrage cost 14 KIA and 43 WIA. On the base's west end L/3/26 engaged a probing NVA platoon at 1950 hours, driving them off dragging their dead, but they left 14 bodies behind. While three main ASPs were maintained, smaller ammunition dumps were scattered throughout the base.

FALL OF KHE SANH VILLAGE

Khe Sanh village and the Huong Hoa District Headquarters 3.5km south of KSCB were defended only by 915th Regional Force Company with two platoons as well as two platoons of Company O, 3d Combined Action Group, together totaling 175 men including five US Army and 20-plus Marine advisors. The NVA attacked the village defenses right after the KSCB barrage began on the 21st. Capt Bruce B.G. Clarke, the army district advisor, initially beat off attacks with artillery brought in almost on top of the defenders. Capt Clarke recalled, "We survived because I continually called VT fuse [airburst] on us and the wire." Calls for air strikes also went out. The 7 Battalion, 66 Regiment, 304 Division attacked from multiple directions using fog for concealment. The village was overrun and the defenders holed up in the district headquarter compound with a CAP platoon 200 yards to the west. At noon the fog lifted and NVA ground attacks dwindled, as continual air strikes were directed against them. The enemy, however, kept up a barrage of mortars and RPGs. Army helicopters managed to deliver some ammunition, kicking it out of the doors over the besieged positions.

Two relief efforts were attempted during the day. D/1/26 from KSCB reached Hill 471 a kilometer north of the village. It was ordered

Besides firing from the simple tripod-mounted DKB single-tube launcher, the 122mm rocket could be barrage-fired from an even simpler mounting, a bamboo bipod. While not as accurate as a tube-launched rocket, all that was required was to man-pack the rockets into a firing area with some electrical wire (usually recovered US field telephone line) and some batteries (often discarded US radio batteries with enough juice left to ignite the rockets). This allowed them to be set up quickly in unexpected locations and fired, with the operators departing the area carrying nothing with them (the bearers having already left).

One of the most commonly used NVA artillery pieces at Khe Sanh was the highly accurate 122mm D74 gun, which had almost twice the range of the US 155mm: 24,000m as opposed to 12,950m.

to withdraw because of overwhelming NVA strength. In the early evening, the Army's 282d Assault Helicopter Company attempted to deliver 50 men of 256th Regional Force Company from Quang Tri City aboard nine helicopters. Mix-ups and confused orders found the unit assaulting into the Old French Fort a kilometer northeast of the village, which was firmly in NVA hands. One helicopter was downed and two crash-landed at KSCB and one at Quang Tri, with the loss of four US KIA and two MIA and about 40 Regional Force troops dead and missing. Early the next morning the separated CAP platoon moved out to fight its way to the district compound, but the NVA had withdrawn and were caught in a B-52 strike.

On the morning of the 22nd, a CAP platoon moved toward the Old French Fort hoping to recover survivors of the failed relief assault. Fearing they were walking into an ambush they withdrew, picking up some 150 weapons from among hundreds of NVA dead. Late in the morning the Marines were ordered to evacuate the village. The Marines on KSCB felt they could not provide consistent artillery support while delivering counterbattery, supporting the hill outposts, and conducting their own patrols. Informed by the Marines at KSCB that they were no longer able to support him, the district advisor relayed this message to

149

The predominant NVA antiaircraft weapon around Khe Sanh was the 12.7mm DShKM38/46 machine gun. The Type 54 was the Chinese version. US troops commonly referred to it as the ".51-cal." Actually both the US .50-cal and Soviet 12.7mm were .51-cal, but the ammunition was not interchangeable as rumored. A 12.7mm antiaircraft platoon protected each mortar platoon around Khe Sanh.

Province Headquarters, which ordered the evacuation of the village. Six helicopter lifts took out all Marines, two Army advisors, and the wounded indigenous troops. Regardless, two of the Army advisors, district government officials (Capt Tinh A Nhi, District Chief), Regional Force, and CAP troops exfiltrated by foot to FOB-3, where they were welcomed. The Marine advisors and Popular Force troops of CAP Company O took up residence there. From that point relations between USSF and the Marines, with the exception of the Marine CAP advisors, began to sour because of Marine distrust of indigenous troops, and because the Marines did not have direct control over the FOB. The remnants of 915th Regional Force Company were lifted to Quang Tri City with their advisors. That afternoon an FOB-3 strike force swept down on the District Headquarters, destroyed everything of value to the enemy, and returned without losses as the NVA was entering the village.

THE BATTLE BEGINS

Dawn of January 22 found KSCB teeming with activity. Another 130 tons of ammunition was delivered by C-123s. They and Marine helicopters were evacuating wounded and refugees, large numbers of whom were flown out January 23–28. Others simply walked out to the east, a perilous trip with many not making it. Damage repairs were under way and marines were digging in. Artillery and air strikes were blasting known and suspected enemy positions. NVA artillery, mortars, and rockets were still hitting the base and outposts intermittently, causing delays to runway repairs and resupply. A helicopter was downed inside the base as it lifted off. At noon 3d MarDiv ordered 1/9 Marines at Camp Evens north of Hue to reinforce Khe Sanh with part of the battalion helicoptered into FOB-3 that afternoon. Greeted by mortar and small arms fire, the battalion took cover wherever it could.

In the morning 1/9 Marines assembled and marched to the Rock Quarry just to the west of the main perimeter. A trail leading to Hill 861

The largest NVA antiaircraft weapon used at Khe Sanh was the Soviet 37mm M1939 based on the 40mm Bofors. The Chinese version was the Type 55. It had a practical rate of fire of 80 rounds per minute. It appears not to have been employed in large numbers.

originated there, and 1/9 would defend the western approach and protect the DZ. The remaining two companies arrived that same day. With only limited building materials, the 1,200-man battalion dug in the best it could and established two outposts.

Activity continued at KSCB, with sporadic enemy shellings destroying the post office and damaging more bunkers and the runway. A fighter and a helicopter were shot down on the 23rd. Marine counterbattery against NVA artillery was proving difficult and only succeeded in expending large amounts of ammunition. NVA artillery, mortar, and rocket positions were extremely well dug in, camouflaged, and spread over such a wide area that targeting was very imprecise.

On the morning of January 24, the 33d Royal Laotian Battalion (BV33) astride QL9 at Ban Houaysan just inside Laos was attacked and overrun by NVA infantry and PT-76 tanks. (BV33 was funded by the CIA under Project "Elephant" and cooperated to some degree with US forces). The battalion fled and arrived at Lang Vei Special Forces Camp with 500 troops and 2,200 dependents and refugees. The USSF positioned them in Old Lang Vei and arranged for food and supplies. Seven tanks were detected by aircraft and one destroyed. This was the first warning that NVA tanks were present. On the same day a Marine patrol one kilometer north of Hill 558 was engaged in a bitter fight, but was able to extract itself.

At the request of Westmoreland for participation by an ARVN unit, LtGen Hoang Xuam Lam, I CTZ commander, contributed the 37th Ranger Battalion. Arriving on January 27, the battalion occupied partly prepared positions on the east end of the perimeter to provide more depth to the defense. The Rangers had to deepen the 2ft wide, 3ft deep trenches and build bunkers and covered trench sections. Through the last week of the month evidence was still being found of NVA preparations for attacks in the way of cut wire and reversed Claymores. The Marines listened for the sounds of tunneling, but this activity never occurred. Air-delivered, unattended ground sensors dropped in surrounding areas monitored enemy movements, and resulted in some success for targeting artillery and air strikes. The scope of NVA activity around the base was becoming apparent. The 3d MarDiv ordered Col Lownds to limit patrolling to within 500m, although 1/9 Marines continued to patrol out 1,200m and FOB-3

FIGHT FOR HILL 861A (pages 152–153)

On February 5, 1968, E/2/26th Marines occupied Hill 861A north of KSCB. The hill was 400m northeast of 861, separated by a saddle. Warned by sensors that a large body of NVA was approaching, they battered it with artillery, but at 0300 hours on February 6 at least 200 NVA attacked the partly prepared position with intense mortar support. Despite the Marines employing every weapon at their disposal, most of the position was overrun. The NVA appeared to be "hopped up" on drugs, and even tear gas failed to deter them. Massive artillery and air support was poured into the valley and the hillside to prevent NVA reinforcement. The NVA, though, appeared to think they were victorious and began looting positions of souvenirs. The lull allowed the Marines to consolidate and they launched a vicious counterattack behind a barrage of grenades, leading to hand-to-hand combat. Within half an hour after the NVA forced their way inside the wire they were driven down the hill. As they withdrew, 106mm recoilless rifles from 558 blasted their ranks. At 0610 hours the NVA attempted a weak counterattack. The company commander, Capt Earle G. Breeding, a mustang officer who had fought in Korea as an enlisted man, coordinated fires from 861, 558, 881S, KSCB, and the Rockpile as well as firing 1,100 rounds from his own 81mm mortars. In the morning over 100 NVA dead were discovered on the hillside and within the perimeter. Many more died further down the hillside and in the valley. The Marine company lost seven dead and 35 wounded; all of the dead were lost in the opening NVA barrage. In retaliation the NVA shelled the outpost and base all day, but Marine replacements were helicoptered into 861A. While artillery and heavy weapons contributed greatly to the battle, it was still a close-quarters infantry fight relying on the infantryman's key weapons. Riflemen were armed with the 5.56mm M16 rifle (1), semi- and full-automatic with a 20-round magazine. The problems encountered with it had been somewhat reduced because proper cleaning methods had been taught. Each 14-man rifle squad had a 40mm M79 grenade launcher (2) firing high explosive fragmentation rounds. Grenadiers were also armed with a .45-cal M1911A1 pistol. A squad with two 7.62mm M60 light machine guns (3) was habitually attached to each rifle platoon from the company weapons platoon. This belt-fed weapon could hammer out 600 rounds per minute. Hand grenades (4), "frags," were essential for defense and were expended in large numbers. M26 frags had a 5m causality radius. The NVA was mostly armed with the 7.62mm AK-47 assault rifle (5), an extremely rugged and reliable semi- and full-automatic weapon with a 30-round magazine. Contrary to persistent rumors, US 7.62mm ammunition could not be fired from it or any other communist bloc 7.62mm weapon. The 7.62mm RPD light machine gun (6) was an ideal assault weapon owing to its light weight and compactness. Its drum magazine held a 50-round belt and could spit out 650–750 rounds per minute. Bangalore torpedoes (7) were used for blasting gaps though barriers. The NVA fabricated their own by fitting TNT blocks end to end and securing them with bamboo strips and cord.

(Peter Dennis)

Troops of 3/26 Marines assemble beside the Khe Sanh runway as they arrive to reinforce the base on December 13, 1967. Little did they know that they would spend the next four months on the base or atop hill outposts.

continued its classified operations locally and inside Laos. The seven-day Tet ceasefire was canceled owing to repeated NVA violations.

On the night of January 30/31, 1968, the Tet Offensive ripped loose through South Vietnam. On the 30th the first B-52 strike in support of Khe Sanh delivered 1,125 tons of bombs. President Johnson's concerns for the base's survival went to the point of discussing the feasibility of using nuclear weapons. While planning never went beyond discussion, it did highlight the president's fears.

On February 5, E/2/26 occupied 861A 400m northeast of 861, as it prevented direct line of sight, and therefore mutual support, between 881 and 558. E/2/26 was then attached to 3/26. That night remote sensors indicated large troop movements west of 881S and Marine and Army artillery saturated the area. At 0300 hours on the 6th, 200 NVA, possibly survivors of the force plastered earlier, attacked 861A supported by mortars. Partly overrun in their incomplete positions, the Marine company counterattacked, resulting in hand-to-hand fighting. The NVA made a weak response and were sent reeling from the hill leaving over 100 dead. The Marines lost seven KIA and 35 WIA.

Scores of NVA 60mm and 82mm mortars ringed the base within 2–3,000m. While the 122mm rocket was accurate in regards to deflection (launcher-to-target line), its range was somewhat erratic. To accommodate this it was preferred to position the launched fire down the long axis of the target. Launch positions east of KSCB would be within range of US 175mm guns at Camp Carroll, and also meant a longer supply line from Laos skirting KSCB. Hills 881S and 861 to the west would have been ideal, but were occupied by Marines. The only alternative was 881N 8km distant, 2km within the rocket's maximum range. NVA 130mm and 152mm guns were dug in and well camouflaged on Co Roc Mountain just inside Laos and 13km southwest of KSCB. Another position was Hill 305 [22] 10km west-northwest of 881S.

Rockets launched from 881N passed over 861, while artillery came over 881S. Even though vegetation, fog, and perpetual dust from air strikes often prevented flash-detection, the rounds were heard and a radio warning flashed to KSCB, "Arty, Arty, Co Roc!" The operator

EVENTS IN CAMP

1. 1700HRS, 6 FEBRUARY. **NVA 152mm artillery strikes the camp from Co Roc Mountain to the southwest.**

11. 0115HRS, 7 FEBRUARY. **The eastern end of the camp is under NVA control.**

12. 0130HRS, 7 FEBRUARY. **Tanks have penetrated the western position of the camp and the MIKE Force outpost is under attack.**

13. 0230HRS, 7 FEBRUARY. **NVA sappers and infantrymen are scattered throughout the camp, but pockets of defenders continue to hold out.**

14. 0245HRS, 7 FEBRUARY. **Tanks are attacking the central perimeter and command bunker.**

15. 0330HRS, 7 FEBRUARY. **The NVA commences concerted attacks on the command bunker. The camp is largely overrun by this time. Small pockets of defenders continue to hold out while other groups break out.**

16. 0335HRS, 7 FEBRUARY. **The Marines deny the defenders holding out in the command bunker their request to send a relief force.**

17. 0430HRS, 7 FEBRUARY. **Concerted attacks continue of the command bunkers. Some of the Vietnamese attempt to surrender and are killed when they emerge.**

18. 0600HRS, 7 FEBRUARY. **The Americans in the command bunker continue to hold out and the NVA is salvaging weapons and munitions from the overrun camp.**

EVENTS

2. 1800HRS, 6 FEBRUARY. **NVA tank companies ordered to move from their assembly areas to attack positions.**

3. 2315HRS, 6 FEBRUARY. **NVA 152mm artillery and 82mm mortars open fire and tanks are in their attack positions.**

4. 2325HRS, 6 FEBRUARY. **9 Company, 198 Tank Battalion with five tanks and 3 Battalion, 101C Regiment attack Lang Vei from the south.**

5. 2325HRS, 6 FEBRUARY. **3 Company, 198 Tank Battalion with four tanks and 5 Battalion, 24 Regiment attack Lang Vei from the west.**

6. 2325HRS, 6 FEBRUARY. **9 Company 198 Tank Battalion with two tanks and 4 Battalion, 24 Regiment attack Lang Vei from the east.**

7. EARLY MORNING, 6 FEBRUARY. **8 Battalion, 66 Regiment attacks Old Lang Vei from northwest. This is a holding attack and is not intended to overrun the Laotian battalion.**

8. 0010HRS, 7 FEBRUARY. **NVA tanks are discovered in the wire on the south side of the camp.**

9. 0050HRS, 7 FEBRUARY. **Artillery fire from KSCB finally begins to fire in support of the camp after disbelieving it was under tank attack.**

10. 0100HRS, 7 FEBRUARY. **Air Force forward air controller arrives over area and commences directing air strikes.**

19. 0700HRS, 7 FEBRUARY. **Dawn and NVA elements begin to withdraw into Laos to the west, though many remain in the area through the morning.**

20. 0800HRS, 7 FEBRUARY. **The Americans in Old Lang Vei direct air strikes in the vicinity of the overrun camp.**

21. 1030HRS, 7 FEBRUARY. **American-led counterattack by Laotian company is launched against Lang Vei from Old Lang Vei, the first of three attempts, all of which are repulsed, with the last attempt made at 1110hrs.**

22. 1600HRS, 7 FEBRUARY. **The survivors in the command bunker breakout and fight their way out of the camp to the southeast. Remaining NVA begin withdrawing to Laos during the late afternoon.**

23. 1700HRS, 7 FEBRUARY. **FOB-3 recovery force air assaults into Old Lang Vei to assist survivors.**

24. 1730HRS, 7 FEBRUARY. **The last survivors are extracted and flown to FOB-3. Indigenous survivors and part of recovery force exfiltrate overland to FOB-3.**

THE FALL OF LANG VEI SPECIAL FORCES CAMP, 7 FEBRUARY 1968

The NVA attack on Lang Vei was a complex and well-coordinated operation, with three combined arms assaults conducted on New Lang Vei from different directions, supporting attacks on Old Lang Vei, artillery support, and ambushes established on QL9 to halt any relief force from KSCB.

Note: Gridlines are shown at intervals of 250m/273yds

QL9

OLD LANG VEI

FRIENDLY FORCES

1 Lang Vei Camp Strike Force with Detachment A-101 in New Lang Vei Camp.
2 MIKE Force Platoon in outpost (platoons are rotated daily).
3 33d Royal Laotian Battalion in Old Lang Vei Camp (8,000 refugees were within 1km).

NVA FORCES

A 9 Company, 198 Tank Battalion with 3 Battalion, 101C Regiment, 325C Division; and two sapper companies.
B 3 Company, 198 Tank Battalion with 5 Battalion, 24 Regiment, 304 Division.
C 9 Company 198 Tank Battalion with 4 Battalion, 24 Regiment, 304 Division.
D 8 Battalion, 66 Regiment, 304 Division.

157

A burning fuel dump set aflame by 122mm rockets. A significant quantity of fuel was stowed on the base for trucks, armored vehicles, weapons carriers, power generators, helicopter emergency refueling, and to burn out latrines – an essential sanitation measure. The bunker in the foreground is built with a stand-off roof above the actual roof with three layers of sandbags stacked atop wooden cargo pallets and set on cable spools for increased protection from artillery, rockets, and heavy mortars.

monitoring the warning net activated a truck horn mounted in a tree and men had 5–18 seconds to dive for cover. The operator would understatedly report back to 881S, "Roger India, Splash," indicating the rounds had indeed landed on schedule.

The close-in B-52 bombardments were "number one on the hit parade" for the Marines. They climbed out of their bunkers to watch the rolling wave of detonations, which were sometimes within a kilometer of the base. Some officers feared the shock waves would collapse bunkers. One Marine described pouring sugar and powdered creamer into a canteen cup of coffee and letting the blast vibrations mix it. An NVA soldier held another view: "B-52 explosions are so strong that our lungs hurt."

FALL OF LANG VEI

Old Lang Vei Special Forces Camp was located on QL9 9km southwest of KSCB and was moved to a new site half a mile to the west in September 1967. While still incompletely constructed, the camp was well bunkered, with established perimeter fighting bunkers. It was manned by 24 USSF, 14 Vietnamese Special Forces, and 443 CIDG including an attached Mobile Strike (MIKE) Force company. Detachment A-101 was under the command of Capt Frank C. Willoughby, but the senior officer present was LtCol Daniel F. Schungel. The camp was well armed with one 4.2in, seven 81mm and 16 60mm mortars; two 106mm and four 57mm recoilless rifles; two .50-cal and 39 .30-cal machine guns, plus 100 LAWs. However, there was little antitank ammunition for the recoilless rifles and no antitank mines.

With BV33 routed and now at Old Lang Vei, four USSF were placed there to aid them. Field grade USSF officers were rotated through the camp as the BV33 commander, LtCol Soulang, would not take orders from a junior USSF officer. On January 30 a USSF NCO accompanying a Laotian patrol was captured by the NVA near Khe Sanh village. On the 31st a CIDG patrol engaged an NVA battalion outside Khe Sanh village, killing 54.

G-12 64ft diameter cargo parachutes descend on the Khe Sanh DZ, each carrying up to a ton of supplies or ammunition. The airdrops were extremely accurate and few missed the 200 x 300m DZ. Recovery crews are already moving out.

NVA units assigned to take Lang Vei received their orders late and were forced to organize on the approach march. The tanks were swam some 10km down the Xe Pon River, on the Vietnam/Laos border, to a point southwest of Lang Vei.

On the evening of February 6, 50 rounds of 152mm from Co Roc struck the camp. At 0050 hours on the 7th the defenders discovered tanks in the wire. The main attack was from the south into the central position by 3 Battalion, 101C Regiment, 325C Division, plus two sapper companies, and 9 Company, 198 Tank Battalion. In addition, 5 Battalion, 24 Regiment, 304 Division and 3 Company, 198 Tank Battalion launched a secondary attack from the west along QL9, with 4 Battalion, 24 Regiment conducting a supporting attack from the northeast. A 152mm battalion of 675 Artillery Regiment and elements of the 7 Engineer Regiment provided further support. The 8 Battalion, 66 Regiment, 304 Division attacked BV33 at Old Lang Vei.

The first penetration was in the southeast compound by five tanks approaching from the south. A USSF NCO destroyed two outside the wire with a 106mm. Four more came down QL9 from the west and two on QL9 from the east. The USSF called KSCB for artillery, arguing with the Marines that they were indeed under tank attack. What the Green Berets did not know was that the artillery on KSCB was being hammered by artillery fire from Co Roc to keep it from firing. Air strikes were also called for. The USSF organized antitank teams, but most of the LAWs either misfired or were duds. One tank was destroyed, but others were crushing fighting positions and NVA sappers blasted bunkers with satchel charges and flamethrowers. Another tank's turret was blown off when its ammunition exploded after it was hit by an LAW beside the command bunker.

Some of the defenders were trapped in the command bunker while the NVA made repeated attempts to flush them out with flamethrowers, satchel charges, and tear gas. Finally, the indigenous personnel surrendered and were executed upon exiting. The Americans continued to hold out. USSF and CIDG were still holding out in other parts of the camp. The three USSF with BV33 convinced some Laotians to counterattack. They continued to direct air strikes and led five counterattacks until two of the USSF were killed. Some USSF and CIDG managed to exfiltrate from the overrun camp. The Marines would not send a relief force as they suspected an ambush awaited them. An FOB-3 reaction force under Maj George Quamo was helicoptered into Old Lang Vei at 1715 hours to aid in the recovery of survivors. With the USSF survivors flown out, some of the recovery force fought their way on foot back to FOB-3. CIDG and Laotian survivors making it to Khe Sanh were disarmed by the Marines and held in a secure area until identified as friendly by USSF. Some 3,000 Montagnard and Laotian civilians and military were flown out on February 8.

Fourteen USSF made it out with only one unwounded. Ten were missing, two of whom were captured. In total 244 CIDG were recovered (61 wounded) and nine Vietnamese Special Forces survived (three wounded). The CIDG was credited with resolutely defending the camp with at least half of those killed dying in their positions. NVA losses were estimated at 250 dead and seven tanks knocked out. All Americans were decorated. Sgt 1st Class Eugene Ashley, Jr. was posthumously awarded the Medal of Honor for his repeated counterattacks from the old camp.

THE FIGHT FOR THE COMMAND POST, LANG VEI
(pages 160–161)

The NVA tank attack on Lang Vei Special Forces Camp began at 0050 hours, February 7 with PT-76 tanks approaching from three directions: five tanks from the south, four more from QL9 from the west, and two on QL9 from the east. The two attacking tank companies each had eight tanks, but only 11 were committed with the rest in reserve. Though a 106mm recoilless rifle knocked out two tanks as they approached from the south, several were soon rampaging through the camp accompanied by infantrymen and sappers. The Green Berets hastily organized antitank teams, but to their dismay they found that most of the M72 light antitank weapons (LAW) either misfired or the round failed to detonate when it struck a tank. The single-shot, throwaway LAW had a 66mm high-explosive antitank (HEAT) warhead capable of penetrating 350mm of armor at up to 200m. This first model was easily affected by heat and humidity; later models were more reliable. Regardless, some functioned correctly and five more tanks were knocked out by the little weapons. Of the seven tanks knocked out, four were recovered by the NVA. LtCol Daniel F. Schungel, a USSF lieutenant, two USSF NCOs, and a Vietnamese Special Forces lieutenant positioned themselves behind a barricade (1) of rock-filled 55gal drums protecting the entrance to the camp's underground 25 x 40ft concrete command bunker (2). A sandbag-faced, concrete observation bunker (3) was situated at the opposite end of the command bunker. It would later be totally destroyed by satchel charges, their blasts so powerful that the sandbags were

blown from the walls and the roof collapsed. An LAW hit set a tank aflame beside the command bunker and the crew bailed out to be shot down by the men behind the barricade. It soon brewed up and its turret blew off. A second tank rumbled past it and was firing point blank into the drums with its machine gun and main gun before it too was hit by an LAW. LtCol Schungel credited Vietnamese Special Forces Lieut Quy's unrelenting suppressive fire with keeping the barricade defenders alive. The cover was destroyed though and the five men, all wounded but one, fanned out with more LAWs and grenades to continue attacking tanks. However, more NVA infantry arrived and they were forced to withdraw into the command bunker. The NVA tried to force the eight USSF, a different Vietnamese Special Forces officer, and a dozen or so CIDG out of the bunker with flamethrowers, satchel charges, and tear gas grenades. Many of the indigenous troops surrendered and were executed as they emerged, but the Americans and a few others held out until the NVA withdrew after daylight. The Soviet-made PT-76 light amphibious tank (4) mounted a 76.2mm D-56B main gun for which it carried 44 rounds of ammunition. A 7.62mm SGMT coaxial machine gun was mounted beside the main gun. A three-man crew was standard, but some in the attack carried four men. The PT-76 was a reconnaissance tank, not a main battle tank. It weighed only 14 ton, not much more than a US M113A1 armored personnel carrier, and had even thinner armor, only 11–14mm, which could be penetrated by a .50-cal machine gun.
(Peter Dennis)

The Marines awarded USSF Detachment A-101 the Presidential Unit Citation (Navy).

The QL9 corridor was now unprotected, making 1/9's position at the Rock Quarry even more important. While the Marines' decision not to send a ground relief force to the camp was undoubtedly wise, the decision did nothing to improve USSF/Marine relations. As an aside, in January a Marine company had practiced a relief effort moving cross-country to Lang Vei rather than on QL9 to avoid ambushes. The operation had required 19 hours in the dense vegetation and rough terrain. A night helicopter relief would probably have been disastrous.

THE BATTLE CONTINUES – LIFE IN THE V-RING

Flush with victory after overrunning Lang Vei, the NVA made its next move closer to KSCB. 1st Platoon, A/1/9, reinforced to 66 men, occupied well-protected Outpost Alpha 1 on Hill 64, 500m west of the Rock Quarry. At 0415 hours, February 8, a battalion of 101C Regiment assaulted up the gentler sloping northwest side of the hillock after a short but heavy mortar barrage. The quarry too was battered by mortar and machine-gun fire. Approaching in the fog and crossing the multiple wire barriers by throwing canvas over them, the NVA overran most of the outpost with the US platoon commander killed fighting back. Less than half the platoon held a trench section on the south side, and they endured endless grenade attacks. A Chinese grenade struck Pfc Michael A. Barry's helmet. He scooped it up, but before he could throw it back it detonated in his hand. His arm, back, and leg were peppered by tiny fragments but his hand was uninjured. A platoon from the quarry counterattacked, assaulting straight into the NVA. Artillery, air strikes, and fire from the quarry blasted the NVA rear to prevent reinforcements and caught them withdrawing from the hill. Over 150 NVA dead were left, while the Marines lost 24 KIA and 27 WIA. The outpost was abandoned as it was too exposed.

February 10 is the date the NVA claim to have switched over to siege tactics. The official NVA history states,

> *Throughout 50 long days and nights, the 304 and 325C Divisions, supported by artillery, antiaircraft artillery, sappers, and engineers from the Route 9 Front, built siege positions stretching right up to the perimeter of the enemy base. Our forces defeated enemy counterattacks and using sniper weapons and artillery attacks, forced American and puppet troops to endure a living hell.*

The NVA now focused on the base itself. Trenching efforts began at this time, approaching from the east and south, reaching 2,000m from assembly areas and sometimes creeping 2–300m at night. Trenches approaching from the east took advantage of the Rao Qung gorge. Heavy bombing and mortars did not deter the digging. Marine patrols would venture out before the fog lifted and fill in or collapse trenches. NVA artillery continued to fire on the base before the fog lifted making

Artillery rounds impacting among the tents. The tents actually protected semi-sunken bunkers from rain. Note the "orchard" of radio antennas in the background, many of which were dummies ordered erected by Col Lownds to deceive NVA gunners.

Lang Vei Special Forces Camp after its fall on February 7, 1968. In the center is the hulk of a PT-76 tank with its turret blown off. Immediately below it is the observation post bunker blasted by demolition charges and its sandbag revetting blown away. To the left of the OP bunker is the collapsed roof of the underground command bunker. The battered 55gal drum barricade can be seen at the command bunker's left end. The south perimeter fighting bunkers of the central position can be seen above the carnage of the command bunker.

it almost impossible for observers to target them. Initially the Marines had tried to blast the NVA at long range, attacking supply lines and assembly areas. It was decided that if the NVA was allowed to sap forward with their trenches, making them more easily detectable and putting them within range of every weapon on the base, it would be easier to attrite them. Marine grenadiers would adjust their M79 grenade launchers on the unoccupied trenches during the day and then lob rounds into them as they were sapped forward at night.

The NVA adopted unusual measures to conceal their artillery. Rather than establish battery positions with four guns closely situated in a geometric position, individual guns were positioned along a common gun-to-target line at roughly 500m intervals. Each gun was adjusted for deflection, and, when a battery fired a mission, an individual gun had only to be adjusted for range. This prevented all the guns from being destroyed in a traditional battery position by a single artillery or air strike. Mortars were sometimes sheltered in deep underground bunkers with a small angled tunnel as a firing port. Theses could then only be fired at a single target hilltop, but it greatly enhanced the survival of the mortar and made it impossible to detect.

The first probe on the 37th Ranger Battalion sector by an NVA company occurred on February 21. Shelling of the base continued with slight increases. On the 23rd, 1,307 rounds, the highest during the siege, killed 12 and wounded 51. ASP 3 blew up, destroying 1,620 90mm gun and 106mm recoilless rifle rounds. On February 25, a B/1/26 platoon south of the base was ambushed in an NVA bunker complex and another platoon was dispatched to assist them, which was also ambushed. The ensuing firefight cost five KIA, 17 WIA, and 26 missing (one of whom was captured). Patrolling was now restricted to that "necessary to ensure the security of … defensive obstacles and local security elements."

Marines are assault troops, aggressive and offensively oriented by doctrine, training, and nature. Khe Sanh was not the kind of situation they desired – dug-in for a prolonged period, enduring constant shelling, and unable to conduct local attacks or even aggressive patrolling.

The "V-ring" is Marine parlance for a rifle target's bull's-eye, and this was how Marines felt on KSCB and the hills. NVA artillery, rocket, and mortar fire fell on the base at an average rate of 150 rounds per day, occasionally reaching over a thousand. The most desirable targets for NVA gunners were the airfield (when aircraft were present), ammunition dumps, and Marine artillery. Natural dispersion of rounds, especially rockets, ensured that no place on the small base and tiny hilltops was safe. Only three Marine guns, however, were knocked out on KSCB and one on 881S, all of which were replaced. The hills did not receive as much fire, though on occasion they were given special attention. Few rockets were fired at the hills because the small size of the Marine positions made them extremely difficult to hit with moderately accurate rockets. Mortars were a greater threat on the hills.

Besides the heavy stuff, the Marines contended with NVA snipers, long-range machine-gun bursts, and sporadic spurts of mortars. All this kept the defenders constantly on edge. Steel helmets and flak vests were mandatory wear. Even "flak pants" were issued, providing diaper-like protection for the groin area. At least one Marine marked on the back of his flak jacket, "Caution: Being a Marine in Khe Sanh may be hazardous to your health" (a quotation from *Newsweek*). The Marines did not take the situation lying down. Life was monotonous on the base and in the hills, and not being the type to turn a cheek they thrived on countering the daily harassment by countersniping with their own snipers, 7.62mm and .50-cal machine guns, 106mm recoilless rifles, and countermortar fire. Observers constantly searched for telltale flashes and smoke to direct artillery, mortar, and air strikes, a difficult task with the fog and hanging dust and smoke.

On 881S Marines were plagued by a particularly good NVA sniper who in a week wounded ten men seriously enough that all had to be medevaced. The glint of his telescope was detected one day and he was dispatched with a 106mm recoilless rifle. His replacement was such a poor shot that that one Marine suggested, "Skipper, if we get him, they'll just replace him with someone who might be able to shoot." While easily detected, he was left alone; a rare instance in combat where his ineptitude kept him alive.

A pair of Marines lay atop their perimeter bunker searching for the faint telltale puff of smoke of a mortar firing. This was extremely difficult among the vegetation, dust, and fog. The three-sandbag-thick roof is laid atop recovered M18 airfield matting. Draped over the sandbags are firing wires leading to M18A1 Claymore antipersonnel mines in the barrier wire.

The daily grind was rough, though: routine monotony shattered with moments of explosions and fear. The perpetual fog and dreariness of the place was depressing enough, though marines commonly described the incongruous beauty of the green hills and the contrasting red soil. The activity was incessant, however: there were constant work details digging trenches, filling sandbags, building and repairing bunkers, repairing wire obstacles, replacing Claymores and trip flares, burning grass in the obstacle belts, collecting and sorting artillery cartridges and ammunition packing materials, hauling trash to the dump, ammunition, water and ration details, scrounging building materials, unrelenting guard duty at all hours, local patrolling, and manning outposts and listening posts. These tasks, coupled with the stress of endless shelling and harassing fire and erratic sleep, was tough to endure for two and a half months. Every marine knew that artillery, heavy mortar rounds, and rockets scoring a direct hit on a bunker would collapse or blow it apart. Every vehicle on the base sported fragmentation holes. Everyone lost buddies when fire struck with little or no warning.

Living conditions were harsh on the base and worse in the hills. Besides all the other work, the marine had to maintain and improve his own position, clean weapons, prepare his own C-rations, and simply try to take care of himself. When the weather closed in, monotonous C-rations were sometimes limited to one or two a day. Often the canned rations could not even be heated. Water was frequently in short supply and rationing was common. Water had to be flown out to the hills; when the weather prevented resupply sometimes each man received only half a canteen cup a day for drinking and shaving, a grooming standard the Marines maintained, though on the water-poor hill positions beards were common. Fog and enemy fire sometimes caused them to go for days living only on a small amount of collected rainwater or dew, and the liquid in C-ration fruit cans. There were no bathing facilities and filthy clothing often remained unchanged, occasionally washed in drums of rainwater. Uniforms, besides being coated with red dirt and dried sweat, were stained with spilt food, coffee, and weapon oil. The soil turned everything red, permeating equipment, uniforms, hair, and skin.

The hilltop Marines lived in grubby, foul-smelling bunkers, which leaked when it rained, and flooded or even collapsed if the earth sides and sandbags became too sodden. They were overrun with rats, roaches, and large green flies (because of so many unburied NVA dead). Latrines had half-55gal drums, which were pulled out daily; the waste was mixed with diesel fuel, and burned generating columns of gray smoke.

While not outright cold, it was damp and chilly with drizzle sometimes lasting for days. To exhausted, dehydrated troops who did not receive field jackets until later in the siege, it was cold much of the time. Rain jackets were worn for some degree of warmth. Field jackets were received later, but there were not enough to go around. Afternoons might be hot and humid. On warm days Marines would wear only flak jackets.

There was no organized entertainment, though Marines often made their own. Tossing footballs or frisbees from hole to hole during shellings (whoever fumbled it had to run out to recover it), tackle football, no touch football, rat-killing contests, and simply reading dog-eared paperbacks were common diversions (with an ear cocked for incoming). After ammunition and rations, mail had priority. "Care" packages from home with food and goodies were shared with buddies. When the Marines' 13-month tour of duty was completed they could be flown out and serious casualties were medevaced out as replacements were flown in. Marines with over six or seven months in-country were even dispatched for out-of-country R&R and returned in a week and a half.

NVA soldiers endured much worse. A soldier of 9 Regiment, 304 Division, wrote in his diary:

> *Here, the war is fiercer than in all other places. It is even fiercer than at Co Roong and Dien Bien Phu. All of us live underground except the units engaged in combat. We are in the sixtieth day and B-52s continue to pour bombs onto our area. If visitors come here they will say that this is an area where it rains bombs. All vegetation and animals, even those who live in deep caves or underground, have been destroyed. One sees nothing but the red earth.*

AIR SUPPORT

Operation *Niagara*, the support of Khe Sanh by air, was absolutely critical, and massive. Resupply, medical evacuation, tactical close air support, strategic bombardment, surveillance, and reconnaissance were all required.

The base was completely reliant on aerial resupply delivered either on a single runway or DZ. On an average day the defenders consumed 126 tons of supplies. Airlift – fixed-wing and helicopter – was more than sufficient to deliver that tonnage and more. After the loss of 1,100 tons of ammunition to NVA shelling, KSCB required a daily average delivery of 235 tons for a while, the peak delivery day being January 27 at 310 tons. Weather sometimes prevented the target tonnage to be met, however, and occasional shortages arose.

On February 10 a landing Marine KC-130F was struck by machine-gun fire. While able to land and taxi off the runway, the transport was aflame and destroyed with the loss of eight of the 11 aboard. Prior to this only seven C-130s had been damaged by ground fire. Another C-130 was damaged on the 12th. The Air Force closed the base to the $2.5 million

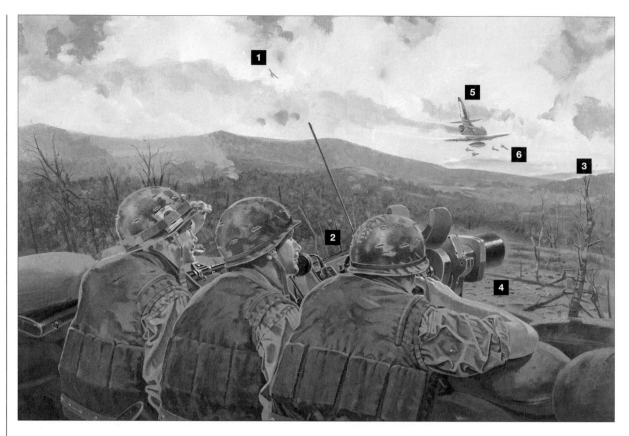

"THE MIGHTIEST CORPORAL IN THE WORLD"
(pages 168–169)

The five Marine hill positions north of KSCB relied on massive air strikes and artillery support from KSCB, and mortar fire from other hill positions. Three 105mm howitzers on 881S were invaluable for supporting the other hill positions and even the main base. Close air support provided by Marine, Air Force, and Navy fighter-bombers was able to deliver a huge amount of ordnance in a small area. An A-4 Skyhawk carried eight 500lb bombs; an F-4 Phantom II could carry up to 24 – twice the load of a World War II B-17G Superfortress; and an A-6A Intruder could deliver 30 500lb bombs. However, F-4s typically carried only 12 500lb bombs to improve performance. Essential to the effectiveness of close air support were the Tactical Air Controllers (Airborne) (TAC(A)), circling all day long in little Cessna O-1E Birddog spotters (1), searching for targets, marking them with white phosphorus rockets, and directing fighter-bombers as they served as the communications link with ground observers. Virtually 24 hours a day fighter-bombers circled in holding patterns as ground and airborne observers searched for targets. When the strike aircraft arrived on-station they reported into the TAC(A) and he would direct them to targets. Standard infantry radios could not talk to fighter-bombers. Infantrymen requested air strikes through the TAC(A), with whom they could communicate using infantry radios such as the AN/PRC-25, the standard back-packed radio. They also used specialized radios such as the VHF/UHF AN/PRC-41 as here (2). Almost legendary is Corporal Robert J. Arrotta

of I/3/26, who controlled over 200 air strikes from Hill 881S, dubbed the "Mightiest Corporal in the World" by his CO. With Lance Corporal Molimao Niuatoa, an American-Samoan known as "Pineapple Chunk" because of his size, he spotted NVA artillery muzzle flashes on Hill 350 (3) using Navy 20-power binoculars (4). The artillery position was 12–13,000m distant and there were no landmarks for reference in the mountainous jungle-covered terrain. He intently kept his eyes locked on the point he had detected the flashes in. No one else was able to spot the weapons' location. Using standard artillery adjusting techniques, "Pineapple Chunk" relayed corrections to the TAC(A) through Arrotta, "Left 2,000, add 1,000" as the Birddog fired 2.75in white phosphorus rockets onto the mountain side. An A-4 Skyhawk (5) would roll in and release its load of eight 500lb Snake-eye bombs (6). A Snake-eye is a standard Mk 82 general-purpose bomb fitted with large Mk 15 folding fins that opened when released to retard the bomb's fall. This allowed low-flying fighter-bombers to exit the target area before the bomb string impacted and prevented damage from its own bombs' fragmentation. The fourth flight nailed the target and the marines were awarded with secondary explosions rippling across the hill's face. The "iron bombs" in use included the 250lb Mk 81, 500lb Mk 82, 750lb M117, 1,000lb Mk 83, and 2,000lb Mk 84. A 500lb Mk 82 was filled with 192lb of Tritonal. Also widely employed was the BLU-27/B 750lb fire bomb filled with 100 gallons of gasoline enhanced and thickened with benzene and polystyrene – Napalm-B for an actual bomb weight of 873lb. (Howard Gerrard)

transports and the Marines followed suit ten days later. C-123s and C-7s could still land. The C-130 ban was lifted for four days at the end of February, but re-imposed when a C-123 was destroyed taking off.

The Air Force first employed the experimental Low Altitude Parachute Extraction System (LAPES) on February 16. This involved a C-130 flying down the runway 5ft off the matting, deploying a special parachute out of the lowered tailgate. Linked-together speed pallets loaded with 9 tons of cargo were pulled out by the parachute, sliding down the runway to a stop. The Ground Proximity Extraction System (GPES) was conducted similarly with an extraction hook attached to the pallet and was first used on March 30: the hook snagged an arresting cable stretched across the runway and the load was pulled out. Because of fog and short visibility only 52 LAPES and 15 GPES missions were conducted.

The primary means of air delivery was by 496 precision parachute drop sorties, where 14–16 1 ton wooden pallet loads could be dropped in a single sortie. Because the aircraft dropped from 400ft and the parachutes opened at less than 100ft above ground, the vast majority of the loads landed in the small DZ with an error of only 95–133 yards. Of the 12,430 tons of cargo delivered to Khe Sanh by the Air Force, two thirds was by parachute, LAPES, and GPES. Marine KC-130Fs delivered another 2,000 tons. Transports actually landing to deliver supplies were on the ground for less than three minutes. As they taxied down the runway, pallets were rolled off the tailgate and any passengers leapt off without the aircraft stopping. Those being flown out, including litter cases, were loaded onto the slowly rolling aircraft as they ran on to the runway from adjacent cover, the able-bodied outbound passengers carrying the wounded. Large numbers of refugees were also flown out by transports. Recovering the pallets dropped on the runway and parachuted onto the DZ was a dangerous job for 3d Shore Party Battalion, Air Force aerial port, and other detailed personnel. Forklifts and trucks were frequently damaged by mortar fire directed at the recovery details.

Resupplying the hill outposts was a major undertaking. Rather than flying in supplies from KSCB that first had to be delivered there by air (the practice prior to the siege), they were flown by Marine helicopters directly from Dong Ha to each outpost and delivered under a hail of automatic weapon, artillery, and mortar fire. This arrangement meant that the helicopters did not have to spend time under the gun at KSCB picking up repacked cargo. It was a slow process, however, as it required 5–10 days for supply requests to be fulfilled. Rather than the outposts providing suppressive fire, as much fire as possible from KSCB was provided so as not to expend outpost ammunition, which would have to be resupplied. The helicopters had to fly to Khe Sanh using instruments and then were directed by radar ground control. Sometimes the base was clear of fog, but clouds enshrouded the hills. Marine Aviation assets were under 1st Marine Aircraft Wing (MAW) commanded by MajGen Norman J. Anderson. Helicopters flown by Marine Aircraft Groups 16 and 36 included:

Bell UH-1E Iroquois (Huey) light utility
Sikorsky UH-34D Sea Horse medium utility
Boeing Vertol CH-46A Sea Knight medium cargo
Sikorsky CH-53A Sea Stallion heavy cargo

Helicopter losses and damage quickly mounted and on February 24 a new system was instituted. The Super Gaggle was a task force of 8–16 CH-

46 helicopters escorted by up to a dozen Marine A-4 Skyhawk attack aircraft and four UH-1E gunships. Air and ground fires were coordinated. A TA-4F would first arrive for a weather check. A-4s would then attack known and suspected gun positions in the vicinity of the outpost with napalm and tear gas spray. Two A-4s laid smoke screens on either side of the approach seconds before the helicopters roared in and four A-4s hit suspected enemy positions. The helicopters dropped their 3,000lb sling loads and were out in seconds. Such efforts sometimes occurred four times a day. Only two helicopters were lost during the hundreds of Super Gaggle missions. Marine helicopters flew over 9,000 sorties delivering 3,300 tons of cargo and 10,600 passengers to KSCB and the hills.

The 3d Air Division's Boeing B-52D Stratofortress strikes, "Arc Lights," were delivered in unprecedented quantities to support Khe Sanh. A single B-52 typically dropped 27 tons of 250, 500, and 750lb bombs. A three-plane cell blanketed a 1 x 2km swathe with 252 500lb and 72 750lb bombs. Safety restrictions limited loads to be dropped within 3km of Marine positions, but as the system was perfected they were delivered within a kilometer beginning on February 26. Once under way, after January 30 eight "Arc Lights" per 24 hours were allocated to Khe Sanh. Later cells arrived every 1–3 hours and, at the peak, two cells every three hours. Target requests required only a 15-hour lead-time. A total of 2,602 B-52 sorties delivered 75,631 tons of ordnance, an average of 35 sorties and 1,022 tons a day, 85 percent more sorties and 82 percent more bombs than the daily average for all of South Vietnam in the prior 12 months. Entire NVA units were destroyed along with fortifications and gun positions; troops deserted. However, they were not fully effective. A Navy lieutenant attached to the Marines, Bernard D. Cole, stated, "The strikes would quiet down the NVA gunners [on Co Roc] for a couple of hours – from the shock … but then they would resume firing." Regardless, Westmoreland credited the B-52 as "the thing that broke their backs …" and no doubt it was.

Tactical close air support delivered by the Air Force, Marines, and Navy was massive. The Seventh Air Force (exclusive of B-52s) delivered 9,691 sorties and 14,223 tons of ordnance, the 1st MAW did 7,078 sorties and 17,015 tons, and Navy Task Force 77 provided 5,337 sorties and dropped 7,941 tons. Douglas AC-47D Spooky gunships with three

7.62mm miniguns firing up to 18,000 rounds per minute were not used over Khe Sanh until March 21 after the air defense threat had diminished.

Two techniques were devised to organize and coordinate combined artillery and air strikes quickly against area targets outside Khe Sanh. These techniques allowed a great amount of fire to be placed on an area much more rapidly than requesting a B-52 strike. When observers, sensors, patrols, or other intelligence detected enemy movements, the Khe Sanh Fire Support Coordination Center went into action. A-6 Intruder attack aircraft, flying from carriers and each carrying 28 500lb bombs, were orbiting on-station, awaiting strike requests. Their run would be controlled by radar on KSCB. Khe Sanh's own artillery and the 175mm guns at the Rockpile and Carroll would plot their firing data based on the target area supplied by the FSCC. Thirty seconds before the Intruders arrived the 175mm guns salvoed 60 rounds into half the target block, the Intruders rippled their 56 bombs into the block's center, and Marine 4.2in, 105mm, and 155mm guns would fire 200 rounds into the other half of the block. The timing of delivery was so precise that the rounds and bombs began to impact simultaneously. The "Mini-Arc Light" covered a 500 x 1,000m block and the "Micro-Arc Light" a 500 x 500m area with proportionally less ordnance. The latter could be plotted faster – ten minutes – and was used for fleeting or smaller targets. The "Mini-Arc Light" required 45 minutes to coordinate. On a typical night three or four "Mini-Arc Lights" and six to eight "Micros" were executed.

Through most of the Khe Sanh operation the 1st MAW and Seventh Air Force, which also controlled Navy air, operated somewhat separately from each other. An agreement was made on January 22 for more effective coordination, but they still functioned independently. The Marines controlled their air support and artillery assets through the FSCC on the base, which included the artillery Fire Direction Center and the Direct Air Support Center. Air Force and Navy aircraft operating over Khe Sanh were controlled by an EC-130E Airborne Battlefield Command and Control Center. The Air Force was dissatisfied with this as they felt 1st MAW assets should have been centrally controlled and available for use anywhere in Vietnam, not just for exclusive Marine use. The Marines, however, considered control of its own air assets essential to their air-ground team concept. The agreement did require the Marines to notify the Air Force of available sorties that they did not require. With rising numbers of Army aviation units deployed to I CTZ and increased tempo and complexity as Operation *Pegasus* got under way, on March 8 Westmoreland appointed Gen William W. Momyr, commanding Seventh Air Force, as the single manager to control all tactical aircraft operating in the Khe

The burned out hulk of a C-123K Provider. Numerous television reporters flew into Khe Sanh for a brief stay, sometimes minutes, and invariably used the wrecked aircraft bone yard as a backdrop for their dire perditions.

Sanh area. Though the integration of all air and control assets did not take full effect until March 22, the coordination of airpower gradually improved.

BEGINNING OF THE END

At 2130 hours on the night of March 1, elements of 66 Regiment attempted to attack the 37th Ranger line, the only determined direct ground attack on the base. Sensors detected the movement and B-52 strikes were diverted along with artillery and air strikes. The first attack was beaten off to be followed by a second two hours later and a third three hours after the second. A total of 78 dead NVA were found in the assault trenches and wire. Many more were killed in the NVA immediate rear, perhaps a large portion of a regiment. Montagnards reported seeing stacks of 200–500 dead NVA. The NVA had assessed the Rangers held the weakest sector and conducted seven probes through March, including one of battalion size on the 18th. The approaching assault trenches were the most extensive in this sector. The Rangers were rock steady and suffered few casualties. Beginning on March 8, the Rangers began sweeps to the east, making two contacts and inflicting casualties on the NVA. Regardless of restrictions on the Rangers entering the Marine lines, B/1/26 (the Ranger's back-up) held them in admiration and a lot of trading went on between the units.

37th ARVN Ranger Battalion troops fight off one of the many probes they endured in February. They are armed with a .30-cal M1919A6 light machine gun. The undermanned, lightly armed battalion acquitted itself well and earned the respect of the marines. (Nguyen Ngoc Hanh)

On March 6 a C-123 was shot down several miles out from KSCB, killing all 49 aboard. Another C-123 was damaged on the runway on the 5th and another was destroyed by mortar fire on the 17th. Three helicopters were also shot down that month. The troops were beginning to feel the strain after two months of shelling and constant stress. It was worse on the exposed hill outposts.

On March 15 various intelligence sources reported signs that the NVA was beginning to withdraw from around KSCB, though indicators of this had been noted on the 6th. NVA propaganda directed at local Montagnards had claimed a final attack would be launched against Khe Sanh, but now the theme was changed to, "Ho Chi Minh would be unhappy if they wasted their time on only 6,000 Marines." On March 22 over 1,000 rounds hit the base and ASP 1 was again struck with 4,000 rounds of artillery and 106mm ammunition destroyed. The next day, 1,109 rounds were received, the heaviest day of shelling for March. Patrols by 1/9 engaged enemy elements on the 24th and 26th, losing eight dead and 21 wounded plus a Huey gunship, while counting 57 dead NVA.

All engagements outside of Khe Sanh had been chance contacts or ambushes to this point. On March 30 B/1/26 executed the first planned attack on an NVA position since the siege had begun. The company launched its attack in the fog at 0755 hours some 300m outside the base. The objective was an 8 Battalion, 66 Regiment trench and bunker complex. Though fog prevented the use of air support, the Marines overran the positions destroying most of the bunkers with demolitions and flamethrowers. NVA counterattacks and heavy mortar fire forced the Marines to withdraw without recovering the 25 missing bodies of the February 25 ambush. They were recovered some days later. The

company suffered ten dead, two missing and 100 wounded, most returning to duty. The action was considered too costly an effort to recover the previous dead, but it did signal the beginning of the end of the siege. The NVA suffered well over 100 dead.

The action on March 30 would be the last significant action of Operation *Scotland I* – it and *Niagara* were terminated on March 31. Much of 325C Division had withdrawn into Laos and 304 was withdrawing to the southwest, though it sent some elements to the north to relieve 325C units. Elements of both divisions remained in the area, however, including artillery. Most of 101C Regiment and detachments from other regiments remained as the main rearguard. Prisoners were reporting low morale and supply problems.

With the Tet Offensive in its dying throes at the end of February, it was not long before consideration was given to the relief of Khe Sanh. There was still mopping up to do after Tet and several major engagements were fought throughout I CTZ.

OPERATION *PEGASUS*

On February 28, LtGen Cushman of III MAF directed MajGen Tolson of 1st CavDiv to re-commence planning for the relief of Khe Sanh. Gen Abrams approved the concept on March 2. A subsequent meeting on the 10th saw the operation codenamed *Pegasus* and the newly formed Provisional Corps, Vietnam was assigned the mission (the ARVN portion of the operation was *Lam Son 207A*). The Corps was assigned 1st CavDiv, 101st AbnDiv, 3d MarDiv, and ARVN elements. The 1st CavDiv was assigned the task of planning and executing the relief. D-Day was set for April 1.

The first step was to build a C-123-capable airfield and forward base, LZ "Stud", just north of Ca Lu, 18km east-northeast of Khe Sanh where the paved QL9 turned into a dirt road. The 1st CavDiv's 8th Engineer, Marine 11th Engineer, and Naval Mobile Construction Battalion 5 built the airfield and would assist with opening QL9. With the airfield nearing completion the 1st CavDiv's 1st Squadron (Air), 9th Cavalry began reconnoitering westward with its scout helicopters on March 25. NVA activity was plotted and clearings for future LZs were blasted in the jungle using delayed-fuse bombs.

On March 30, the 3d MarDiv and 1st ARVN Regiment launched a divisionary operation northeast of Dong Ha. The 1st Marines, brigade-sized 3d ARVN Airborne Task Force, and 26th Marines were attached to the 1st CavDiv, the 26th in order to expedite coordination for the relief. This collection of 20 infantry battalions was the largest III MAF operation to date. H-Hour was 0700 hours on April 1, but weather closed in, grounding the helicopters upon which the operation depended. Regardless, 2/1 and 2/3 Marines began their thrust down QL9 with 1/1 securing LZ "Stud" and the 11th Engineers clearing mines and obstacles and repairing bridges, culverts and bypasses. With weather lifting at 1300 hours 3d Brigade, 1st CavDiv launched its three battalions aboard helicopters to secure LZs "Cates" (5/7) and "Mike" (1/7, 2/7) north and south of QL9 about halfway to Khe Sanh. Artillery was flown in and was in position to support the next day's operations by nightfall. Contact with the NVA was very light. The 320 Division did fight some engagements in an

effort to keep QL9 closed, but even the official NVA history admits that their antiaircraft defenses were inadequate to deter the 1st CavDiv.

The pace then picked up. Between April 2 and 4 the 1st CavDiv's 2d Brigade leapfrogged past the 3d and established LZs "Wharton" (1/5, 2/12) and "Tom" (2/5) south of QL9 and southeast of Khe Sanh, while 3d Brigade's 2/7 set up on LZ "Thor" just to their east. The battalions began probing northwestward. On the 4th the usually aggressive 1/9 Marines thrust out from the Rock Quarry 2.5km to Hill 471 above Khe Sanh village. Attacking the hill at 1500 hours, it was in their hands at 1600, but at a cost of ten KIA and 56 WIA with only 16 NVA dead left behind. The 7 Battalion, 66 Regiment counterattacked before dawn the next morning, but wasted itself leaving over 140 dead and five prisoners. The Marines lost only one KIA and 28 WIA. Meanwhile, 1st Brigade, 1st CavDiv swung deeper south and established LZ "Snapper." On April 6, G/2/26 ventured out from Hill 558 to clear the 861 ridge finger pointing toward KSCB. The day's action cost the company four KIA, 47 WIA, and six missing (later recovered), but claimed 48 dead NVA.

The 1st CavDiv battalions southeast of Khe Sanh continued to advance and the 1st Marines continued to clear QL9. On the 6th 1/5 Cavalry met stiff resistance at the Old French Fort and was relieved by 2/5 the next day. Also on the 6th, 2/12 Cavalry was air-assaulted onto 571 to relieve 1/9 Marines, the first contact by Khe Sanh defenders with a relieving unit. Then 1/9 advanced northwest toward 552 and 689. D/1/26 pushed out of KSCB on the 6th to the south to recover the bodies of 21 Marines missing since February 25. The NVA were rapidly breaking contact and opposition dwindled. The 84th Company, 8th ARVN Airborne Battalion was helicoptered in to link up with the 37th Rangers at 1350 hours, making this the first reinforcement on the base since the 37th itself arrived on January 27.

On April 7, 2d Brigade, 1st CavDiv secured the Old French Fort and Khe Sanh village. On the 8th 5/7 Cavalry airmobiled in 500m south of the base, walked up the road, and shook hands with 1/26 Marines. The 3d Brigade airlifted its command post into KSCB at 0800 hours and relieved the 26th Marines of base defense responsibilities. There was little fanfare, just a "ho-hum" attitude as the Marines only wanted to shift into the offensive. While the siege had been wearing on the defenders,

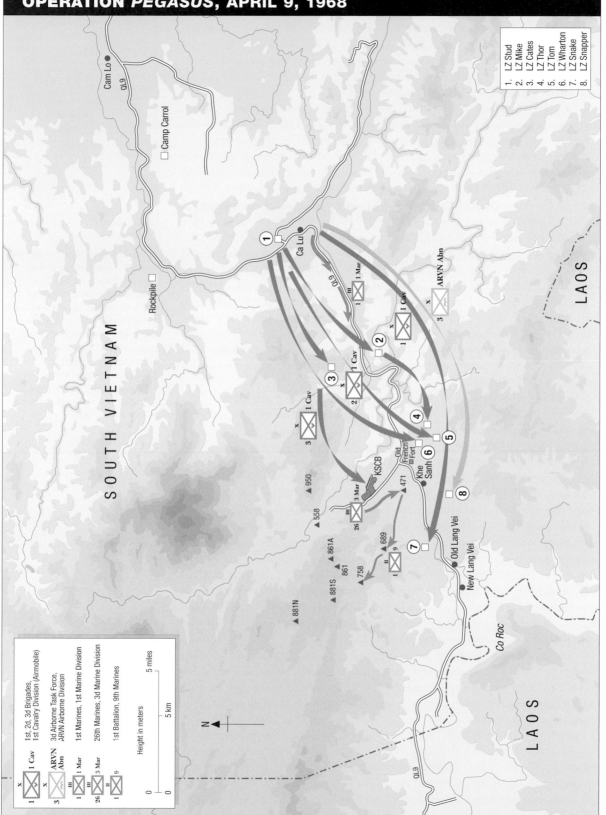

Cam Lo

QL9

Camp Carrol

Rockpile

S O U T H   V I E T N A M

Ca Lu

1. LZ Stud
2. LZ Mike
3. LZ Cates
4. LZ Thor
5. LZ Tom
6. LZ Wharton
7. LZ Snake
8. LZ Snapper

1 Mar

1 Cav

ARV'N Abn

1 Cav

1 Cav

1 Cav

3 Mar

KSCB

Old French Fort

Khe Sanh

471

689

▲ 950

▲ 558

▲ 861A

▲ 861

▲ 881S

▲ 758

▲ 881N

Old Lang Vei

New Lang Vei

Co Roc

L A O S

L A O S

N

1 Cav — 1st, 2d, 3d Brigades, 1st Cavalry Division (Airmobile)

ARV'N Abn — 3d Airborne Task Force, ARVN Airborne Division

1 Mar — 1st Marines, 1st Marine Division

26 Mar — 26th Marines, 3d Marine Division

1 9 — 1st Battalion, 9th Marines

Height in meters

0 — 5 km

0 — 5 miles

177

there was no feeling that they had been "saved." The 1/9 Marines first secured Hill 552 then 689, which had dominated their position in the quarry for so long, but at a cost of nine KIA and 27 WIA by mortars, without making direct contact with the NVA. The 3d ARVN Airborne Task Force moved into LZ "Snake" near Lang Vei on the 8th and began clearing QL9 to the Laotian border after a hard fight between 3d ARVN Airborne Battalion and NVA rearguards.

No enemy artillery fire fell on KSCB on the 9th, and ARVN paratroopers secured the abandoned Lang Vei site. LtGen Rosson of the Provisional Corps informed LtGen Cushman of III MAF that resupply drops were no longer necessary and the airfield was open to all traffic. Rather than resupplying *Pegasus* forces from LZ "Stud", the ammunition stockpiles on KSCB began to be issued to allow their reduction before closing the base. On April 11 the 11th Engineers completed opening QL9 to Khe Sanh, constructing nine bridges, 17 bypasses, and rebuilding 14km of road. Khe Sanh was now linked by ground to the outside world for the first time since July 1967. That same day most of the 1st CavDiv was alerted to prepare to assault the A Shau Valley to the south and units soon began departing, as did the 37th Ranger Battalion. Col Bruce F. Meyers, formerly commanding Special Landing Force "Alpha" afloat off the coast, relieved Col Lownds on the 12th after nine months at Khe Sanh. By now Marine patrols were pushing out from the hill positions and making light contact. Graves with hundreds of NVA dead were found along with abandoned individual and crew-served weapons, some vehicles, and masses of munitions and supplies.

On the night of April 13, 3/26 left 881S and occupied assault positions on the south slope of 881N. A provisional battalion weapons company was left on 881S to provide fire support and security. Artillery and mortars battered 881N all night. Launching their attack at 0530 hours, followed by a massive artillery barrage on the crest, marines seized 881N at 1428 hours with a loss of six KIA and 21 WIA, while finding over 100 dead from 8 Battalion, 29C Regiment plus three prisoners. Regardless of the NVA withdrawal, that day a C-130 was destroyed on the runway by rocket fire.

Westmoreland declared, "It was clear … that the base had outlived its usefulness. We now had the troops and helicopters to control the area … and we had the logistics and a secure forward base at Ca Lu to support these operations." Both Generals Cushman and Rosson prepared plans to evacuate Khe Sanh based on Westmoreland's statements. However, at a commander's conference on April 15, Westmoreland stated that the force in the area would continue operations. Most of the forces would not be redeployed nor the base closed.

Pegasus was terminated at 0800 hours on the 15th and Operation *Scotland II*, the continued defense of the Khe Sanh area, was initiated. Free World losses for *Pegasus* were 51 US Marine, 42 US Army, and 51 ARVN KIA plus 667 wounded from all three services. NVA dead by body count was 1,304 (although estimated NVA dead totaled 3,500–5,000) plus 13 prisoners. Huge caches of supplies and munitions were captured.

To control units in the area, Task Force "Glick" was formed under BGen Jacob E. Glick, Assistant Commander, 3d MarDiv. He too was prepared to close the base and arrived with a minimal staff and had to plus up for continued operations. Task Force "Glick" included 1st and 26th Marines, 1/9 Marines, and 2d Brigade, 1st CavDiv – ten battalions.

A **Super Gaggle** flight of CH-46A "Purple Foxes" make a run into a hilltop position. The netted cargo sling would hit the ground, the crew chief would immediately release the cargo hook, and the chopper lift off in seconds. This sling load carries plastic-lined, steel 155mm propellant tubes filled with water. The tubes were plentiful and survived dropping from a low height.

The 1st Marines began helicoptering into KSCB on the 16th and the 3d ARVN Airborne Task Force departed for Hue. That same day A/1/9 was engaged southwest of 689, the battalion's position, and pinned down. Company C was sent to reinforce the beleaguered company and it too was pinned. Company D was committed and found itself in a serious fight. The new battalion commander ordered the companies to withdraw late in the afternoon leaving their dead. He was unaware of the division order that every effort would be made to recover the dead. The last elements did not close on the battalion position until 0300 hours and found there were 20 KIA and 15 missing. Two helicopters with recovery teams landed in the battle area the next day and were immediately engaged. One helicopter actually landed on and killed an NVA soldier, the enemy were so thick on the ground. The force was driven off with one of the aircraft crash-landing in the battalion perimeter. Army helicopters subsequently recovered two live Marines in the area. Most of the missing dead were recovered on the 22nd. This final disorganized fight by the defenders of Khe Sanh did not have a good ending. It cost them 41 KIA, 32 WIA, and three missing. The battalion commander was relieved, but a corporal was awarded the Navy Cross.

On the 18th the 26th Marines turned over control of KSCB to the 1st Marines under Col Stanley S. Hughes at 0800 hours. The 26th Marines and 1/9 were airlifted to Quang Tri City and Dong Ha where they were given five days' rest and recovery. Many of the troops were bitter when they learned Khe Sanh would be abandoned. What had they endured 77 days for? Why had so many died for a place that would be given up? These were age-old questions of warfare. Others just did not care. Many in the upper echelons finally admitted, though they gave other rationalizations, that the position was simply too remote and exposed, and too difficult to support with the enemy more easily able to supply its forces in the area. Others had warned of this. Also, Khe Sanh's usefulness as a launch site for the projected invasion of Laos had passed with the commencement of the Paris peace talks.

Scotland II continued until February 28, 1969 with patrol contacts, ambushes, and occasional shellings. The 1st Marines were assigned 1/1, 2/1, 2/3, and 3/4 Marines for this mission. The NVA remained active in the area, but at greatly reduced levels. In May, increased 308 Division activity was discovered south of Khe Sanh and Operation *Robin* was conducted, but these post-siege actions are beyond the scope of this book, with one exception.

CLOSING KHE SANH

ARVN Rangers man their ragged, hastily prepared, outer perimeter during an NVA probe. The officer talking on the AN/PRC-25 radio has the ARVN Ranger snarling tiger's head painted on the front of his helmet. Visible weapons include a 40mm M79 grenade launcher and 7.62mm M60 machine gun. (Nguyen Ngoc Hanh)

The decision to finally evacuate Khe Sanh was made on June 1. Ten days later Westmoreland departed Vietnam and General Creighton W. Abrams took over command of MACV. LZ "Stud" at Ca Lu would become the northwestern-most base in an effort to shorten supply lines, consolidate mobile operations, and control the tri-border area through reconnaissance-in-force. The 1st Marines would secure Khe Sanh as 3/9 Marines and Company A, 1st Engineer Battalion would not only evacuate supplies and material, and dismantle the base, but also raze it. Nothing useable would be left for the enemy. The 3/9 served as a work force and they was augmented by detachments of the 3d and 11th Engineer and 3d Shore Party Battalions. Seabees from Naval Mobile Construction Battalion Unit 301, the same unit that had improved and extended the runway almost a year before, would recover the matting – this was Operation *Charlie,* which was commenced on June 19 by Task Force Hotel with the 1st Marines.

Some 800 bunkers and positions were dismantled and buildings torn down or burned. Hundreds of thousands of sandbags were slit and spilled. Three miles of concertina barriers were either recovered or bulldozed into trenches and backfilled. Vehicle hulks and damaged equipment were cut up with torches and buried in pits to deny the enemy propaganda displays. Much of the material (lumber, timber, picket posts, concertina wire, runway matting, base equipment, etc.) was hauled to LZ "Stud", now redesignated Vandegrift Combat Base, for reuse. As a last measure the barren and blasted red earth was dusted with tear gas powder to discourage NVA scavengers. The last convoy out was on July 5 and 3/4 Marines officially closed Khe Sanh Combat Base with a brief flag-lowering ceremony at 2000 hours. Engineers at the tail end of the convoy removed tactical bridging behind them on QL9 on June 6.

There was some final action at Khe Sanh. When it became apparent to the NVA command that Khe Sanh was being evacuated, it was expected that at least some small-scale attacks would be conducted in order to claim the NVA had driven the Americans out and overrun the base. On July 1, I/3/4 engaged an NVA unit in the vicinity of the Old French Fort, killing over 200 with a loss of two KIA. The 1/1 Marines remained in the vicinity of the former base for a week, picking off scouts and scavengers. The last fight was on Hill 689 where missing Marines were recovered with a loss of 11 Marines and 89 NVA killed. Finally, 1/1 was loaded aboard helicopters with their dead and the remains of seven previously missing Marines and lifted off for Quang Tri City.

The official NVA history stated:

On June 26 1968, the enemy announced he was withdrawing from Khe Sanh. Our armed forces rapidly tightened their siege ring, mounted shelling attacks, suppressed the enemy's efforts to transport troops by helicopter, and conducted fierce attacks to block the overland route, forcing the enemy to prolong his withdrawal … On July 15 1968 our soldiers were in complete control of Khe Sanh.

Regardless of the inflation of their final actions at Khe Sanh, the NVA was now in control of a strategically important area and its lines of communication were extended further into South Vietnam.

The radio relay site on 950 was turned over to the ARVN, and as Hickory Hill it remained in operation until it was overrun on June 5, 1971.

15 tons of cargo is spilled out of the tailgate of a C-130E "Herkybird" from 400ft. The low altitude and delayed opening of the parachutes allowed extremely good accuracy on to the small DZ. The French dropped from much higher altitudes.

22 Named Hill 305 as it was on an azimuth of 305 degrees from Hill 881S.

AFTERMATH

Casualties suffered by both sides at Khe Sanh have long been disputed, with much debate over the figures. Part of the problem lies in the specific timeframe, area, and units to which figures were "credited" to Khe Sanh. Some figures count the casualties for Operation *Scotland I*, which ran from November 1, 1967 to April 15, 1968 and includes a period of almost seven weeks prior to the siege commencing on January 20. Other figures are listed for the period of the 77-day siege, January 20–April 15, 1968, but the most quoted figures only cover January 20–March 31 and count casualties from April 1–15 as part of Operation *Pegasus*, even if incurred on the base. Casualty figures were usually restricted to those suffered on KSCB, the hill outposts, and on patrols in the base's immediate vicinity. Casualties for operations *Pegasus* and *Scotland II* are counted separately.

The fiercest debates revolve around simply who was counted. The most frequently quoted figures are those supplied by the Marine Corps. These figures, however, only count Marines and assigned Navy medical personnel in the immediate Khe Sanh area. Those who were not included in the Marine totals come to a significant number of casualties:

US Army, Air Force, and Navy Seabees on KSCB
US Army, Air Force and Navy aircrewmen in the immediate Khe Sanh area
FOB-3 US and indigenous troops
37th ARVN Ranger Battalion
US and RF/PF troops at Khe Sanh village
USSF and CIDG troops at Lang Vei
33d Royal Laotian Battalion
C-123 shot down on March 6 several miles out from Khe Sanh with a loss of 49 occupants

Precise figures are not available for all of these categories. Approximately 70 other US non-Marine personnel were killed at Khe Sanh (this does not include aircrewmen lost in the area). At Lang Vei eight USSF were killed and three captured while some 200 CIDG were killed or taken prisoner. ARVN Ranger, RF/PF, indigenous FOB-3, and Laotian losses are not known.

The Marines lost 205 KIA between January 20 and March 31. However, when individual Marine unit losses are totaled the figure comes to 274. It appears that 1/9 was not included in 26th Marines totals. "Charlie Med," the KSCB medical unit, records 2,541 treated: 2,037 WIA and 490 non-battle injuries. No figures are available for non-battle deaths. A total of 2,249 wounded/injured were evacuated and 292 returned to duty. It is suspected that these are only Marines and possibly other US wounded/injured, but does not include the various categories of indigenous personnel.

In regards to both operations *Scotland I* and *Pegasus*, one source gives the total US causality count for both operations as 730 KIA, 2,642 WIA, and

1967 Pre-siege US and NVA Casualties, Khe Sanh

Action	To–From Dates	Marine			NVA		
		KIA	MIA	WIA	KIA	Probable	POW
Hill Battles	April 24–May 14	168	2	443	940	1,500	6
Operation *Crockett*	May 15–July 16	52	1	255	204	350	2
Operation *Ardmore*	July 17–October 31	10	0	24	113	225	0

seven missing, and an ARVN count of 229 KIA and 436 WIA. is not certain what categories of US personnel were actually included nor does it address non-ARVN indigenous personnel (CIDG, RF/PF, SOG commandos).

Actual NVA casualties are of course unknown and can only be estimated. Official NVA histories never mention their own casualties. The Marine body count of enemy casualties since *Scotland I* commenced on November 1, 1967 was 1,602 dead, seven prisoners, and two defectors. Estimates of overall enemy dead, however, were 10–15,000, though it has been questioned whether it was as high as this, considering the low strength of the two divisions and other units committed. It is recognized that rear support units suffered heavy losses and that replacements and units from other divisions may have been committed, but the actual losses may have been on the lower side of the range.

Thousands of Montagnard, Vietnamese, and Laotian refugees were flown out of Khe Sanh during the course of the siege. Here Vietnamese rush to load a C-123K. Only the "K" model was used at Khe Sanh, as its rocket-assisted take-off capability was necessary to help it climb steeply and quickly out of antiaircraft range.

The NVA's official history claims:

During the 170-day siege[23] *of Khe Sanh we eliminated from the field of combat 17,000 enemy troops (including 13,000 Americans) and destroyed or shot down 480 aircraft of all types. Our forces at Khe Sanh successfully fulfilled their mission of drawing in and tying down a large enemy force (which at its largest totaled 32 battalions, 26 of which were American, representing one-quarter of all the US combat battalions in South Vietnam ...*

The small communist monument at Khe Sanh today claims, "112,000 US and puppet troops killed and captured. 197 airplanes shot down." These claims of course are absurd. A total of only 16 US and four ARVN battalions were committed to Khe Sanh and *Pegasus* together.

The 26th Marines, and attachments, were awarded the Presidential Unit Citation (Navy) for their performance at Khe Sanh from January 20–March 31, 1968. The media's fanciful doomsday predictions were unfulfilled.

---

23 The NVA viewed the "siege" as lasting until the base was evacuated in June 1968.

FURTHER READING

Braestrup, P., *Big Story*, Boulder, Colorado (1977)

Corbett, John, *West Dickens Avenue: A Marine at Khe Sanh*, Presidio, Novato, CA (2003)

Ewing, Michael, *The Illustrated History of Khe Sanh*, Bantam Books, New York (1987)

Fall, Bernard B., *Hell in a Very Small Place: The Siege of Dien Bien Phu*, J.B. Lippincott, Philadelphia (1966)

Hammel, Eric, *Khe Sanh: Siege in the Clouds, An Oral History*, ibooks, New York (2004)

Karnow, S., *Vietnam: A History*, New York (1983)

Kellen, K., *Conversations with Enemy Soldiers in Late 1968/Early 1969: A Study of Motivation and Morale*, RAND Corporation (1970)

Krulak, Victor H., *First to Fight*, Naval Institute Press, Annapolis, MD (1984)

Luong, Colonel H., *The General Offensives of 1968–69*, US Army Center of Military History, Washington (1981)

McCoy, James W., *Secrets of the Viet Cong*, Hippocrene Books, New York (1992)

Murphy, Edward, *The Hill Fights: The First Battle of Khe Sanh*, Presidio, Novato, CA (2003)

Natly, Bernard C., *Air Power and the Fight for Khe Sanh*, US Air Force, Washington, DC (1973)

Nolan, K., *Battle for Hue: Tet 1968*, New York (1983)

Oberdorfer, D., *Tet!* Garden City, NY (1971)

Pearson, Lt Gen Willard, *The War in the Northern Provinces 1966–1968*, Vietnam Studies, Department of the Army, Washington, DC (1975)

Phillips, William J., *Night of the Silver Stars: The Battle of Lang Vei*, Naval Institute Press, Annapolis, MD (1997)

Pisor, Robert, *The End of the Line: The Siege of Khe Sanh*, Norton, New York (1982)

Prados, John and Ray W. Stubbe, *Valley of Decision: The Siege of Khe Sanh*, Houghton Mifflin, Boston (1991)

Pribbenow, Merle L. (translator), *Victory in Vietnam: The Official History of the People's Army of Vietnam, 1954–1975*, University Press of Kansas, Lawrence, KS (2002) (Originally published as *History of the People's Army of Vietnam, Vol. II*, Military History Institute of Vietnam, Hanoi, 1994.)

Shore, Capt Moyers S., II, *The Battle for Khe Sanh*, Headquarters Marine Corps, Washington, DC (1969)

Shulimson, Jack, LtCol Leonard A. Blasiol, Charles R. Smith, and Capt David A. Dawson, *US Marines in Vietnam: The Defining Year, 1968*, Marine Corps Vietnam Series, Headquarters Marine Corps, Washington, DC (1997)

Son, Lieutenant-Colonel P. (senior editor), *The Viet Cong Tet Offensive 1968*, Saigon (1969)

Spencer, Ernie, *Welcome to Vietnam, Macho Man: Reflections of a Khe Sanh Vet*, Corps Productions, Alamo, CA (1991)

Stanton, Shelby L., *Anatomy of a Division: The 1st Cav in Vietnam*, Presidio, Novato, CA (1987)

——, *Vietnam Order of Battle: A Complete Illustrated Reference to U.S. Army Combat and Support Forces in Vietnam 1961–1973*, Stackpole Books, Mechanicsburg, PA (2003)

——, *The Rise and Fall of an American Army*, Presidio, Novato, CA (1985)

Stockwell, David B., *Tanks in the Wire: The First Use of Enemy Armor in Vietnam*, Daring Books, Canton, OH (1989)

Stubbe, Ray W., *Khe Sanh: The Final Formation*, privately published, (1995). (Available from Ray Stubbe, 8766 Parkview Court, Wauwatosa, WI 53226)

Telfer, Maj Gary L., LtCol Lane Rogers, V. Keith Fleming, Jr., *US Marines in Vietnam: Fighting the North Vietnamese, 1967*, Marine Corps Vietnam Series, Headquarters Marine Corps, Washington, DC (1984)

Windrow, Martin, *The Last Valley: Dien Bien Phu and the French Defeat in Indochina*, Weidenfeld & Nicholson, London (2004)

INDEX

Figures in **bold** refer to illustrations